Definitive Guide to Running a Successful REIA Meeting
With A National Speaker

Contact the authors for speaking engagements

For additional information on hosting webinars, courses on CD's and DVDs, and more, see page 191.

Shaun McCloskey:

www.lifeonaire.com
135 Triad Center West, O'Fallon, MO 63376
Office: 314-966-0656 ext. 111
Fax: 314-966-5554

Topics Covered:

−Short Sale Real Estate Investing
−Debt Free Real Estate Investing
−Lifeonaire Living (How to Create a Business that Serves Your Life)
−How to Become a Top-Selling National Speaker (and Craft a Killer Presentation that SELLS!)

Larry Goins:

www.LarryGoins.com
4607 Charlotte Hwy. Suite 1, Lake Wylie, SC 29710
Office: 803-831-0056
Fax: 803-831-0805
Larry@LarryGoins.com
For bookings contact Kandas@LarryGoins.com

Topics Covered:

−Wholesaling
−Automation
−Marketing
−Software and Websites for Investors
−Seller Financing
−Virtual Investing
−Private and Hard Money and More

DEFINITIVE GUIDE TO

RUNNING A SUCCESSFUL REIA MEETING

WITH A NATIONAL SPEAKER

Everything you need to know to find the right Speaker, promote the event, fill the room, make money AND have your members love you!

SHAUN MCCLOSKEY & LARRY H. GOINS
IN COOPERATION WITH NATIONAL REIA

Published by The Goins Group, LLC
4607 Charlotte Hwy. Suite 1
Lake Wylie, SC 29710

Book cover design by Killer Covers
Email: vaughan@killercovers.com

Book interior design by Jean Boles
http://jeanboles.elance.com

CONTENTS

FOREWORD

Revenue-generating Real Estate Speakers, or "Gurus" and local Real Estate Investor's Associations (REIAs), often have the exact same goals, although they view them from differing perspectives.

Each has the ultimate goal of helping as many individual investors to succeed as possible by providing high quality, usable information. This is generally accomplished by product sales, which generates needed revenue for the operating expenses and profit for each.

So, since we are both after the same thing, why is it that at times working together and nailing down specific working agreements and procedures is no easier than wrestling a greased pig? The answer, it seems, is lack of knowledge about the different perspectives of each group.

For this very reason, Larry Goins, long-time Real Estate Investor, National Speaker and former Metrolina REIA President, and Shaun McCloskey, Lifeonaire Founder and Real Estate Expert, with the National Association of Real Estate Investors, have collaborated to produce a set of "best procedures" for local REIAs and speakers working together. Inside these pages is a boatload of valuable information that will help each to effectively "stand in the shoes" of its counterpart and view things from that perspective. This information is sorely needed and long overdue, and it provides a welcome roadmap to smooth future working relations.

JC Underwood,

Executive Director of Metrolina REIA and former President of National REIA

Shaun McCloskey

Shaun McCloskey is a seasoned real estate investor, author, coach, and owner of Lifeonaire REIA, a for-profit real estate investor association located in Shaun's hometown of St. Louis, MO. He's been investing for over a decade and has completed somewhere north of 300+ real estate deals, consisting of just about every kind of investing strategy you can imagine. Widely known for his expertise in pre-foreclosure flipping, Shaun has also been a featured speaker at many of the top REIAs in the country. In 2014 he co-authored a life-changing "Amazon Best Seller" book entitled *Lifeonaire*, which is designed to help business owners to not only make money, but also to have a life in the process. He is the author of a number of home study courses on the subject of real estate investing and speaking and is considered "the Coach's coach," having coached a number of high caliber business and real estate coaches across the country.

Shaun and his wife, Jennie, have three children, Lucas, Norah and Elise. They are members of The Crossing church in Chesterfield, MO. He also plays lead guitar and sings in a band—just for fun! His personal and business motto is "give first."

Larry Goins

Larry Goins, from Lake Wylie, South Carolina, is an active real estate investor who is currently buying 10-20 properties per month without ever leaving his office. He has bought properties in 11 different states.

He has written two books that can be found in bookstores. His first book, *Getting Started in Real Estate Day Trading*, teaches how to buy houses and sell them the same day using the internet. His latest book, *HUD Homes Half Off,* teaches how to buy HUD houses at 50, 40 even 30% of list price. Larry is also the author of several home study courses as well as automation tools used by investors.

Larry travels the country, speaking and training audiences about his strategies at conventions, expos and Real Estate Investment Associations. In the past, Larry has served as President (2003 & 2004) of the Metrolina Real Estate Investors Association in Charlotte, NC, a not-for-profit organization that is a local chapter of the National Real Estate Investors Association.

On a personal note, Larry and his wife, Pam, have two children, Linda and Noah. He is a member of New River Community Church in Lake Wylie, SC and occasionally plays guitar in the Church Praise Team. As a husband, father, businessman and real estate investor, Larry holds true to his core values and moral integrity. His personal and business motto is *"People & Principles before Profits."*

PREFACE

Why We Wrote This Book:

We wrote this book because as we travel across the country, we have both often seen a disconnect between the speaker and the REIA group. Although they both have the same common goal, they seem to go about trying to reach it differently. We want to unite the speaker and the group and lay everything out on the table so both can see things from the others' prospective. We hope this book will allow you, the reader, to have more profitable events with larger attendance, to increase memberships, and to have better relationships with the speakers that you book for your meetings.

What You Will Learn And Gain From This Book:

This book will show you marketing strategies that some of the biggest promoters use to fill their events. You may not use all of them, but you will surely use some of them. The best part is using the techniques in this book to fill your events and meetings will also help you increase your membership and your revenue.

Chapter 1:

What Makes An Organization Swim In Success Vs. Drown A Slow Death?

Booking a speaker for your REIA event can be one of the most exciting (and most profitable) things you've ever done for your organization. If done correctly, not only will you and your audience learn an overwhelming amount of the best, most up-to-date real estate investing information on the planet, you should also exit the event with a substantially larger balance in your REIAs bank account. Bringing in a national speaker can increase attendance at your meetings, provide a new spark of energy in the room for a new and exciting form of investing, and can just downright be a fun experience. Of course, that's if it's done right. Done wrong, however, and it could be one of the worst experiences of your life, and the life of your REIA could dramatically suffer.

I immediately think of a national speaker who was brought to my local REIA many years ago. Not only did he show up late, he also showed up with a strong scent of alcohol on his breath. And when I say strong, I mean it smelled like someone dipped his entire body in a barrel of Jack Daniels—for a month! His presentation started with a few rather rough comments (or should I say, insults?) towards women, then followed with a 10 minute story about how his wife left him a few years earlier for another man. He then went on and on about how you just can't trust anyone, and he was even kind enough to let the audience know that he was not, in fact, drunk. Instead, he was on some pain medication for a bad knee. I found it rather fascinating that he started limping immediately after he made that last comment. It was almost as if he had forgotten his knee problems right up until the point where he made that statement. Interesting how that worked...

Needless to say, not only did this particular speaker end the night with a big goose egg as far as sales go, he also ticked off a lot of really good REIA members; some never came back to another meeting again.

Before we jump into the event-changing lessons within this book, let me make one thing clear: If you're the leader (or one of the leaders) of a Real Estate Investors Association, everything that happens (or doesn't happen) at your REIA is a direct reflection on YOU! This means:

- How you run your REIA is a direct reflection on you.

- Who you book as a speaker is a direct reflection on you.

- Whether or not the speaker is well received is a direct reflection on you.

- How many people showed up to the meeting is a direct reflection on you.

- Whether or not the event was a success is a direct reflection on you.

- Whether or not the event was profitable is a direct reflection on you.

That being said, (and before those comments freak you out a bit), there are a lot of things you have control over in this equation. We (Shaun and Larry) have collectively spoken at hundreds of different REIAs around the country, and trust us when we say we've seen what works and what does not. Sometimes the difference between a well-run, insanely profitable REIA and one that's on the verge of bankruptcy is very minor differences in leadership. Sometimes the differences are more obvious. But the bottom line is, every REIA that we've seen has room to take their businesses to another level.

Everyone can improve, and even small improvements added up equate to huge differences in results.

Transversely, not addressing the small things that need improvement can lead to the exact opposite results. I personally watched one REIA, with more than 600 paid members and averaging more than 300 attendees at each monthly meeting, in just six months, dwindle down to less than 50 members showing up to meetings each month. I've seen this happen more than once.

How is this possible? you may ask. Well, there are a lot of factors that played in the demise of these organizations. We'll get into details throughout this book, but for right now, just know that not only can a REIA's reputation become compromised rather quickly by booking the wrong speakers, it can also be compromised by booking too many speakers, selling too hard, and not providing enough good, solid content.

A well-run REIA is a shared responsibility. The REIA owner or leader has a responsibility to provide overwhelming value to the people that show up every month. Everyone else that is involved in the REIA should be there to help facilitate and make this happen. It doesn't matter whether we're talking about a national speaker, the guy setting up the tables, the staff that operate the sales table at the back of the room, the guy that sets up the audio, or the volunteer helping to check in new members. Everyone's role within the REIA should be built on the same foundation—provide overwhelming value to everyone that shows up to every meeting, every month. Pull this off and you'll have the best REIA in town.

Many people think that there is some sort of secret recipe and that the few who know the ingredients to this recipe aren't willing to share it. Well, we've got good news for you—not anymore. You have the secret recipe right in your hands.

Does this mean that the only purpose of the REIA is to provide overwhelming value? Well, yes and no. Providing overwhelming value is certainly the key to getting people to not only attend this month, but to also come back month after month. But there is a second ingredient that is just as important:

Your REIA Must Be Profitable.

Make no mistake about it, your REIA must generate income. Don't apologize for this. And why try to limit it? The truth is, your REIA should make as much money as possible without apology. Of course, this is only under the condition that you've already met the first purpose, which is to provide overwhelming value. One of the quickest ways to ruin a REIA is to forget either one of these two purposes. Despite what you may think, your members know the difference too. If you're part of a REIA that puts profitability first above all else, your members can and will smell it a mile away. In that situation, it becomes obvious that the owners care nothing about the profitability of their members and are only concerned about filling their own pocketbooks. Conversely, if a REIA owner is so concerned about providing overwhelming value that they never get around to considering the importance of making a profit, that association is equally doomed.

There is nothing wrong with a REIA making money, and lots of it. Some of you have a different belief, and we're here to challenge you on this. A well-run REIA group provides hundreds of thousands if not millions of dollars of revenue for their members and the community each and every year. Think about it... every rehabber who uses the information gained by attending your REIA to renovate houses, spends money on contractors, supplies, employee wages, taxes, all of which benefit the community—not to mention that the rehabber himself is making great money applying what he's learned at your association. And that's only a rehabber! We haven't even mentioned landlords, lenders, title companies and the countless other types of people, or shall we say "vendors," that your REIA will help to make profitable this year. Not only is it okay to charge money for providing this level of overwhelming value, you're robbing people the joy of implementation if you don't charge them for it!

If you think for one minute that you can provide your members with everything they could possibly ever need to run their business in a single 90-minute REIA meeting each month, you'd better think again. Your members need more. They want more. They're willing to pay for more, and the worst thing you can do for them is to hold on to the false belief that there is something wrong with providing all of these things and charging for it. We provide some of the best real estate investing training on the planet, and neither of us apologizes for charging for it. As a matter of fact, if we didn't charge for it, people wouldn't value it, they wouldn't implement it, and they wouldn't ever get to experience the benefits of implementing all they've learned.

The truth is, if done correctly, it is possible to have the best of both worlds. Our goal with this book is to teach you how to provide overwhelming value to your members, provide incredible education, and also make more profit than you thought possible. And we have had the experience of working with just about every kind of REIA you could possibly imagine. We've worked with a REIA that makes more than one million dollars per year and is growing like crazy. We've also worked with REIAs who used to be that big and are dying a slow painful death. Which one would you rather lead?

So What's The Difference?

I've spoken at two different REIA organizations in the same week. I gave the exact same presentation to the exact same size audience at each separate organization. I felt great about both presentations. At one REIA, I sold just "okay," while at the second one, I blew it out of the park and had record sales. Why do you think this is?

There are a lot of factors that we'll get into throughout the course of this book, but you should know that more is not always better.

Some REIAs feel the need to have a selling speaker at every meeting, every single month of the year. At first glance, it might make more sense to have more selling speakers to generate more income; however, that's the exact opposite of how it works in the real world.

We equate this way of thinking to the shoe store that's just not selling enough shoes. The shoe store owner thinks to himself, "I'm just not making enough money. There must be a better way!" So in an effort to make more money, he raises the prices of all of his shoes by 50% thinking that if he only sells the same amount of shoes he's been selling in the past, his profit will go up substantially and he'll be a much happier business owner. Unfortunately, this way of thinking doesn't necessarily take into consideration what really works. This approach may make sense on paper, but the reality is that raising prices alone actually alienates the few customers he had coming to his store. Now, even the old customers stop coming altogether, irritated that shoe prices skyrocketed for no reason. No extra value was provided, just higher prices.

Many REIA owners have the shoe store owner mentality, and try to solve their cash-flow challenges by having more selling speakers each year rather than focusing on a handful of really good ones. The shoe store owner should have never increased prices, at least, certainly not without providing more value than he was previously. Instead, he should have increased the value perceived by each existing customer and increased the amount of customers coming in to the store each day. Instead of raising prices, perhaps he should have spent a little more time, focus, and even money, giving people a good reason to even come into his store, then providing them with evidence that proves he's got the best shoe store around.

The very best REIAs in the country (those that have the highest rate of returning members as well as the highest profit potential) don't focus on picking a large volume of national speakers each year. Instead, they have anywhere from three to six of the very best selling speakers each year (six is on the high end; most of the best REIAs have four). At first glance this may not appear to make the organization more profitable since there are less opportunities to sell from the front of the room; however, your members will get burned out if every month they're hearing sales pitch after sales pitch. While I'm all for a good sales presentation, even I don't want to hear one at every meeting.

If you pick the right speakers to come to your REIA, the audience won't even know they're being sold to. A good speaker will provide a presentation where not only a lot of people run to the back of the room with their money in hand dying to buy the product, a good speaker will also provide enough value to the rest of the audience so that even the non-buyers feel like their time was well spent. More on this later—but yes, there is an art to this, and it's unlikely that a non-experienced speaker will understand how to do both. People are tired of the same old dog and pony show. They want real value. They want excellent training. They're willing to pay for it, and your job is to give them what they want.

There are many variables to running a profitable REIA as well as choosing the right speaker to co-host your events, and we'll cover each of them in detail in this book. Marketing is important. So is the environment you create within your REIA. So is your introduction to the selling speaker before each meeting. So is what was done at last month's meeting. So is what's going on at next month's meeting. So is how the sales table is operated. So is how the tables are set up in the room for your members. All these things and much more play a role in the impact and profitability your REIA. So let's begin, shall we?

What NOT To Do

One thing I won't do for you (or should I say to you) throughout this book is to blow smoke up your hind end. I hear horror stories from speakers all the time about what a REIA owner or president did that killed sales—and the REIA owner didn't even know they did it!

For example, my good friend, Steve Cook, recently spoke at a REIA in Wisconsin (I don't dare name names here, but if you're reading this book, you know who you are), and the problems started before he even began speaking. The promoter (REIA owner) lied about how many people attend their meetings each month. When she called Steve to get him booked months ahead of time, she swore they usually have 70-80 members in attendance each month. When Steve showed up ready to speak, there were less than 20 people in the room (18 to be exact). Steve found it interesting that they normally have 70-80 each month even though there were only enough chairs in the room to seat 30 people max. Not only that, but there wasn't even any additional space to put more chairs in the room if by some chance a miracle happened and more than 30 people showed up. But it gets better. Steve went through his entire 90 minute presentation, had everyone in the room hooked on his content, then at the very end he provided a way for the audience to extend their education beyond the 90 minutes. He offered up his home study course and three-day-live flipping event for sale.

As soon as he finished his close (the part of the presentation that says, "Ok, for those of you ready to take it to the next level, join me at the back of the room to sign up right now..."), there were three people headed to the back table with credit card in hand ready to purchase. Just then, out of nowhere, the promoter jumped up, grabbed a microphone and said, "No guys, WAIT! We forgot to do the raffle drawing. Everyone sit back down so we can finish up the raffle! Steve, you can help pick the winning ticket!"

Naturally, everyone did as they were told and sat back down while she proceeded to give away three or four items that no one cared about. Steve tried to remain calm, knowing that what had just happened was likely going to ruin his chance of selling anything that night. When she was finished the drawing, all of the momentum that Steve worked so hard building over the course of his 90-minute presentation was completely gone. He went from what was going to be at least three sales to ending up with zero sales, all because the promoter didn't just keep quiet and let him finish his official close. Who did that hurt? Was it just Steve? Of course not; it also hurt the REIA club. Two simple mistakes made for an unsuccessful meeting. The first was the lie about attendance. The second was the forfeit of what little sales Steve would have pulled together out of such low attendance.

Here's your first shocking truth: REIA owners lie about their attendance. Often times, they'll tell a speaker they have more in attendance each month than they actually do. It happens all the time. (Don't hate the messenger; hate the message.) But the flip side of the coin carries another shocking truth—speakers lie about how well they sell. Yep, I said it. It's true. It happens all the time, too. Speakers will often tell the REIA club about their absolute best-case scenario of sales that they may not be able to duplicate on a regular basis. Here's the real truth though—neither of these lies are necessary. Both lies only end up doing more harm than good.

Needless to say, Steve didn't have nice things to say about his experience at this particular REIA. In the REIA owners' defense, no one had ever told her about the importance of keeping quiet when the speaker is doing his or her closing. But that one thing killed what was already going to be low sales because of low attendance.

By the way, in an attempt to keep things easy, if I refer to a speaker as "he" going forward, you should know that this is not an attempt to be sexist in any way; I use only one gender to keep from going back and forth, making it easier for the sake of writing and for you, the reader. That's what's going to happen from now on. I'm not worried about being politically correct here. I'm more concerned with making sure you "get" what you need to get to have an awesome association this year. Okay? In the same context, we may use the term "we" or "I" or any other similar term to refer to us at any given time. Moving on...

How about my friend, Anthony Chara? Anthony shared a story with me once about a REIA with about 100 or so members in the audience that he spoke to a few years ago. Towards the end of his presentation, he did a closing strategy where he would build up the value of his offering to tens of thousands of dollars' worth of training, then he would ask the the audience, "If all this did was make you an extra $50,000 this year, how much would this course be worth to you?" As he told me the story, he shared with me how normally no one wants to be the first one to speak up, and he's prepared for this. He said that he simply asks the question, knowing there's going to be an uncomfortable silence, and then he just sits back and waits for a response. He said that sometimes it's 5-10 seconds of absolute silence, and he does this on purpose. Eventually, someone always speaks up and shouts out a number that's a lot more than he's getting ready to sell his product for in his final close. Under normal circumstances, it's worked well for him and served its purpose of building up the value of his offer in the minds of the audience. Only this time, it backfired on him. This time, after about four or five seconds of uncomfortable silence, someone from the audience shouted out, "Just say the F-ING price already!!!"

Anthony couldn't believe what he'd just heard. It threw him totally off track. He had done that portion of his close dozens of times in the past, and it had always worked to his advantage. Only this time it backfired terribly. So much so, that it flustered him, and he had a hard time finishing the closing portion of his presentation.

Finally, the night was over, and Anthony was in the car headed home. As he was driving, he got a call on his cell phone from the

REIA owner who wanted to call and apologize for what took place in his REIA meeting that night. During his heartfelt apology, he said, "I don't know what I was thinking when I yelled that out from the back of the room... I'm sorry."

Yes, you read that right. It was the REIA owner that yelled "Just say the F-ING price already!!!" Anthony was floored. I don't know know who was more shocked—Anthony when that happened to him or me when he shared the story with me for the first time. Funny story, yes, but again, it was detrimental to sales that night. Everyone suffered as a result of one bad move.

I was at a REIA group not too long ago which was fairly close to my home town in South Carolina, so I agreed to go speak although they advised me there would only be between 30-50 in the room. I was to go on at 6:30 pm. Well at 6:30 there were about 10 people in the room, so they delayed the start of the meeting, hoping more would show up. This delayed me going on until 7:30. Just before I was to go on, the group leader asked the audience who would like free local coaching. Then he had someone get up and give a testimonial about his coaching and about how you didn't need any other kind of training. He then had them go to the back of the room and set up a time for a one-on-one meeting.

After that was over and he got ready to introduce me he said, "Here is a guy that has a system very similar to mine (he was also getting into the speaking business). Please welcome Larry Goins."

Now why would they want to even listen to me if they were getting free coaching and my system was very similar to the group leaders'? Needless to say, it was a disaster for both of us, even though they eventually had eighteen in the room.

One last story and then we'll get into the specifics, step by step. I was personally speaking at an event once in California. This was a pretty well run REIA group that had been around for many years.

Unbeknownst to me, the REIA owner, during his usual announcements at the beginning of the meeting, introduced a woman who was going to speak for a few minutes before me. This woman proceeded to get up in front of the group and share information about her local coaching program. It ended up being a ten-minute pitch on why local coaching was so important and why people should consider her as their real estate coach and mentor. She went on to say how no one in the room should ever listen to advice from anyone that doesn't live and operate their entire real estate business in California, because the laws are drastically different there than anywhere else in the country. She insisted that people who listen to those "out of towners" end up doing it wrong and usually end up in JAIL or worse—putting their students in JAIL! She went on to justify many more reasons why people should only choose to learn from local investors, and she then said, "Thank you," and turned the mic over to the REIA owner again. The REIA owner then said, "Okay guys, now we're ready for a very special guest, all the way from St. Louis, Missouri, please welcome Shaun McCloskey!"

Now I've got two major challenges to overcome. First, I was not informed that there would be other speakers that night, and a big part of my closing offer and product package was to include four months of coaching as a bonus for the first certain amount of people that signed up. The woman before me, however, threw me under the bus, saying that my coaching is no good because I clearly don't live in California. Not only that, but remember, "you will likely end up in JAIL if you listen to an out-of-towner," right?

The only thing I could do to break the ice was to be fast on my feet. I started the presentation with, "Thanks for having me everyone! I'm excited to be here all the way from St. Louis. This is the first time I've been allowed to leave the state of Missouri in a while, because I tried doing business here in California once, and as a result, I've been in PRISON for the last 10 years!" Of course, I said it as sarcastically as I could without trying to make the other speaker look too bad. But I had to address this right up front, since everyone in the audience was thinking about it, and there was no way around it. The truth is, the speaker didn't leave me many options. Everyone had a good laugh (including me), and I was able to move on. But the truth is, had this happened to a non-experienced speaker, it would have most definitely killed sales that night.

Again, this was a small mistake that was not intentional at all, but did it have an impact on sales? In this particular case, it didn't negatively impact my sales because I was fast enough on my feet to overcome the objection. But many speakers wouldn't have been able to overcome that barrier. It could have cost me, and the REIA owner, a lot of money in sales that night.

Chapter 2:

How To Book An Incredible Super Awesome Speaker For Your Event

Why Even Book A Speaker?

REIA groups exist primarily for education and networking. These are local and regional groups made up of real estate investors who are looking for opportunity around every corner. While each group may have its own focus (some will be more focused on land lording while others may be more focused on flipping), the members will always be interested in learning more about real estate and how they can increase their earnings. There are also many speakers that have strategies and ideas that maybe no one in your local group is taking advantage of.

Expert Knowledge

It goes without saying that a good speaker is going to share some pretty incredible knowledge and experience. Rather than every individual student learning what to do and what not to do the hard way, they can shave years off of their learning curve by hearing from someone with experience. The truth is, reading books and watching videos cannot replace a live person standing in front of the room sharing their hard earned, first-hand knowledge. When I give a short sale presentation, I often start out the presentation with an example of the very first deal I did back in 2003 (wow, has it really been that long?), where I made just about every mistake you can possibly make. For the sake of keeping this book under 1,000 pages, I'll save you the gory details of everything I did wrong in that first deal, but in the end, I ended up losing a grand total of $86,000. That really stung! But the lessons that came from my experience on that deal make a huge impact on people to this day. I'm happy to report that I haven't lost money like that on a deal since then, but the lessons that came from that first deal can't be taught in a book. It takes someone sharing their real life stories and sometimes even their own personal pain and anguish to ensure that the student really "gets" it and doesn't make those same mistakes. Conversely, I also share, step-by-step, how a student of mine made $275,000 on one flip transaction, and how they can do the same thing. All they have to do is follow the recipe. And believe me, there is a recipe for how to make that kind of money on a deal just like there is a recipe to lose $86,000 on a deal, too.

Every good speaker has a great story to share. Some provide education on what to do. Some provide an example of what not to do. In either case, there is something magical that happens when the audience feels what the speaker has experienced through the power of a moving story. It's in this way that the audience member can really grasp the lesson within the story without having to go out and lose $86,000 on their own deal. After hearing a story like the one I share, they know exactly what not to do, and they are thankful that someone shared these tools and strategies with them up front rather than them having to learn it on their own. As a matter of fact, I often hear how much the audience appreciates my willingness to be vulnerable in the front of the room and "tell it like it is," since this is how most people feel they learn the most.

Many speakers have an expert level of knowledge about real estate investing that they are more than happy to share. This knowledge was gained through years of trial and error out in the real world. Not only have they put basic theories to the test, they've likely developed a number of their own strategies and techniques as well. Booking a speaker like this will give your REIA group a unique opportunity to learn directly from the source. They'll be able to pick up information that they may not find elsewhere, while having the chance to ask specific questions.

Niche Expert Knowledge

It's one thing to know how to flip a real estate deal. It's another thing to know how to flip a vacant land deal. And it's another thing to know how to flip a vacant land deal that is a high-end ocean front property in the $3-$10 million price range.

While some speakers will cover the general real estate market, many speakers focus on a particular area in real estate where they've become an expert and created a successful business, and this can provide a wealth of information to your members. This expert level of knowledge can often be quite specific as well. There is a lot that goes into real estate investing, and it can often help to understand it from a different point of view. I hear people in REIAs often describe themselves as "in the real estate business." Really? Does that mean you're a real estate agent? A contractor? A house flipper? If you flip houses, does that mean you're a rehabber? A wholesaler? A short sale negotiation expert? When you say you flip houses, do you buy them and flip them? Or just put a note under contract and flip the note? There are many roads we can go down in the real estate world. Sometimes having a niche speaker opens up the eyes of the audience to really see how many different opportunities there are in the world of real estate investing.

Not every REIA speaker needs to be a nationally recognized real estate mogul. People such as landlords, property managers and Section 8 experts can all help round out the knowledge base of any group. The information these speakers provide is invaluable and will allow your group to get a unique and detailed perspective of very specific avenues within the wider world of real estate.

Some REIA groups also have a specific focus. One group may, for example, consist of investors who are interested in purchasing foreclosed properties. Bringing in a foreclosure attorney can be a great way to educate the group about legal pitfalls and the current state of the market. This is someone who can provide incredibly valuable education for a group with such a niche interest.

Promoting The Group

Even though each REIA group may have a different focus, they all share the same concern. As a group, they must continue to grow if they want to be successful. This means it's vitally important to make sure people know about the group so they can attend the events and eventually become a member. Before they think about joining the group, however, they'll want to know if it's a legitimate and active organization.

Most REIA groups meet on a regular basis, but these meetings don't generally bring in many new members. Events such as expos, seminars, and promotion of speakers are what fill the seats. Booking a speaker can be a great way to generate some interest in a group. Many people will attend the event just to hear the speaker and will end up joining the group because they enjoyed the event so much. The speaker and the REIA both benefit from this.

If you're booking the right types of speakers, the speaker will also partake in the marketing to help promote the group (and the event itself). Most speakers will have already put a significant amount of time and money into promoting themselves. They likely already have websites, mailing lists, and extensive search engine optimization which guarantees them a good spot on search results. When you book this speaker, you will essentially be tapping into this established promotional machine. This means a good speaker will cross promote speaking at your event. Not every speaker gets this concept, but the good ones do.

I had a speaker once tell me, "Why would I promote people to come to this particular group that asked me to speak? They're already on my email list. If I promote to my list that they should come to the REIA meeting where I'm speaking, I'll have to split any sales with the REIA." This is not the speaker you want coming to present at your association. This is what's called "scarcity mentality," and not only is it unnecessary, it's just flat out wrong to take this approach. The way I figure it, if I'm speaking in Portland, Oregon, I want every student I have to know when and where. Some of them will travel for miles just to see me speak there, and yes, some of them will buy my product during the presentation. This does, in fact, mean that I'm going to be splitting some of what I would be selling them with the REIA, but it's a sale that I wouldn't have even gotten without the student seeing me live from the front of room anyway! The way I figure it, everyone wins!

Another sign of a good speaker is if he is willing to promote the necessity of being a member of the REIA during his presentation. That's one thing I learned a long time ago. REIAs love it; the students need it; and it only takes a few minutes to pull off if done correctly. The speaker at the front of the room holds a certain amount of authority just by being at the front of the room. When I'm speaking I'll usually mention something that sounds like this; "How many of you are current members of this association? Good! This REIA is so important to the success of each and every one of you! I can't highly recommend enough that each one of you become a member tonight if you're not one already. The only way to be successful in today's real estate market is to surround yourself with other people who already are successful; so be sure to join tonight, and when you do, I have a free gift that I'd like to give you just to show my support for what REIAs like this do for investors like you." By the way, I can say this from the front of the room because I firmly believe it!

The speaker will want to inform their readers and subscribers of the event and will generally link to your group, sending new people to the group's website. When someone does a search online for the speaker's name, some of the results will contain information about your group. Simply put, booking a speaker can be a great way to advertise your REIA group and increase the attendance of an event. You can essentially ride the coat tails of your speaker's own personal marketing. It's effective, and it works.

One of the things we have also done with groups is to agree to split the cost of a direct mail campaign. Most speakers already have a mail piece or post card designed and should agree to split the cost of doing a direct mail campaign to get more attendees to the meeting. You can mail to your list and the speaker's list of those that are close by. This is also a great way to increase attendance.

Profits For All

While education and gaining new members are important considerations, money is (and should be) one of the biggest concerns of many groups. Just like any other organization, a REIA group needs to make enough money to support itself. Most groups will do this in a number of ways, such as membership fees, selling tickets to events, and offering a range of products for sale.

The most obvious financial benefit to booking a speaker is attendance. A popular speaker, assuming he has a desirable topic and effective marketing materials (more on that in a minute), will fill seats and sell tickets. With the right speaker, a rather small group can see a surprisingly large attendance list and will be able to make a very nice profit by selling tickets to the event.

I remember a while back, there was a REIA that was just getting their feet wet. Two gentlemen bought an existing REIA from another owner who could never seem to get more than about 50 people to a meeting. These two new owners brought in a national speaker that had quite an extensive marketing plan, and they worked together to implement it over the course of about 30 days. When the speaker came to the freshly owned REIA for their first meeting, there were almost 300 people in the room. This was before I started speaking, and I remember sitting there in awe, wondering how they were able to fill so many seats so quickly. It was quite simple. This speaker had been around the block a few times and knew what attracted people to a live event. He was willing to share this with the REIA, knowing that it would benefit both of them in the long run, since it would provide more potential new members to the REIA and would also provide a larger audience (and therefore more buyers) for the speaker. Granted, the speaker knew he was going to end up splitting these sales with the REIA, but he didn't have the *scarcity mentality*. Instead, the more he shared, the more he also received. It was a win-win, and it worked perfectly. I have since implemented many of the same strategies, and to put it simply, marketing works. You just have to implement it.

When you book a speaker, you are also booking a sales opportunity. The speaker is there to make money, and when they do, you will make money as well.

It can be hard for a REIA group to generate a healthy revenue, but there is nothing better than having a speaker come in and promote books, courses, videos, and more. When you consider the increased attendance a speaker usually brings, it becomes clear that an event like this can be a fantastic sales opportunity which simply can't be replicated by other means.

Different Events For Different Speakers

The first step in booking a speaker is to determine the type of event at which they'll be speaking. Most REIA groups will have regular monthly or even weekly meetings. These are often fairly basic, and the audience will consist mostly of regular members. While this may not exactly be an "event," it can still be a good opportunity for a speaker if they are just sharing knowledge and experience.

Other REIA groups may have a sub-group which has a specific focus. These meetings will have a niche-specific audience, and so they will want to hear a certain category of information from a speaker. Once again, these meetings are not necessarily a huge sales opportunity, but inviting speakers on a regular basis can help to continue to provide value to your REIA and improve membership numbers.

In addition to the regular meetings are actual events. These are a big deal and have often been in the planning stages for a considerably longer time than a typical REIA meeting. The audience may include people who have never attended a REIA meeting, but were drawn in through effective marketing and the chance to hear from the speaker. This could consist of a separate event altogether, or it could be tied to a regular REIA meeting, but what makes this different is the amount of time and marketing that goes into filling the room.

An event like this could be an all-day event on a Saturday. The audience will be there for a number of hours, mainly listening to the speaker and possibly asking questions. (Whether or not a speaker will take questions during his presentation varies from speaker to speaker. Make sure you ask the speaker how he wants to handle this so you can help facilitate if need be.) A lot of the audience may be unfamiliar with the strategies being taught because these events are designed to grab the attention of the newbies that have little or no experience in real estate investing. A speaker for an event like this needs to be dynamic enough to keep the audience's attention focused for an extended period of time. They must be able to provide enough information to keep people from getting bored and distracted. Nothing is worse than spending your entire Saturday with a speaker that sounds like the history teacher on *Ferris Bueller's Day Off*. "Bueller? Bueller?"

Some REIA groups may also plan much larger events. A weekend long seminar, for example, is a popular option which requires a significant investment of time. It is the perfect length for an in-depth discussion of certain topics, but it can also have a few hidden pitfalls. An entire weekend event is quite a long time for one speaker to host, and not every speaker will have the skills needed to perform for so long. If you're planning an event like this, make sure your speaker has experience—and lots of it.

Other events can be huge and somewhat chaotic. Expos are possibly the largest event a REIA group will ever put together. They can be fun, exciting, and a wonderful way to meet new people while making some money at the same time, but they also require a ton of planning, people, and organization to pull off successfully. There is currently one each year that takes place in Ohio, called the OREIA Convention. Google it and you'll see what I'm referring to. It's a four-day event that takes place in the 3rd quarter of each year. During the convention, anywhere between ten to twenty national speakers are usually brought in to speak. There are typically two seminar room presentations going on at any given time throughout the four-day event, and each speaker typically speaks at least twice. Then on the final day they typically have two headliners that speak for four to six hours each. An event like this may last all weekend (or more) and will have a large variety of different speakers and topics. It's important to make sure the speakers won't contradict each other and that each one is professional and experienced.

There are also some non-traditional events, such as buying tours. This is where a REIA group will hire a bus and then drive around, checking out properties and making offers. Since there will be plenty of time on the bus, you may consider having someone who can speak a bit come along on the trip. This is, however, a vastly different situation than sitting in a room, so you need to make sure your speaker is comfortable with it. Although this type of bus tour isn't always the best environment for selling products, it can be an excellent environment for selling properties.

The bottom line is to book a speaker who is right for the event. Each event will have a different time frame and a different dynamic. Someone who is great at giving a two hour presentation may not do so well if they need to speak all day. Conversely, a speaker who has mostly handled weekend long seminars may not be able to condense their information down to a few hours. Always keep the type of event in mind when searching for a speaker.

So How Do You Differentiate The Good Ones From The Bad Ones?

Finding The Right Speaker

Knowing how to find the right speaker for your group is important because a bad speaker can have a seriously negative impact on the group. When you book a speaker you're tying the reputation of your group to what this person says and does. If your speaker is using foul language and is only there to sell their own products, your members will feel cheated, and this will reflect back on your group.

Before you even begin considering a speaker, you need to understand what constitutes a good candidate. There are a lot of people who will offer to do a speaking event, but only a few of them are any good. The following criteria will help you weed out the bad speakers and choose one which will help bolster your REIA group.

Does Their Reputation Precede Them?

Reputation goes a long way in the real estate investing business, especially if you're a speaker. The real estate community is actually smaller than most people think, and both good and bad news travels fast.

One of the first things to consider is how recognizable your potential speaker is. Every industry has its rock stars, and these people will be known throughout every level. Not only have they been successful on an individual basis, they've been able to work with others to help them become successful as well. Speakers like these may be in high demand, but they will also be the ideal candidates for your REIA event.

Booking a well-known speaker with a track record will make every other step easier. Because they are already recognizable, promoting the event will be much easier than it would be if booking a speaker that has little to no experience speaking or promoting. This person will have a large base of their own fans and customers which they can leverage to increase attendance at the event. When they promote the event, they are essentially endorsing your group to this huge audience, which can lead to new members and an increased interest in the group itself. Of course, you never want to base your attendance of your event solely on whether or not the speaker can draw his own crowd, but it certainly helps to have this as a starting point.

When choosing a speaker for your event, a great way to gain some insight about his past performances is to ask him what he liked best about the last three events in which he spoke. If you want to hear how easy or difficult a speaker is to work with, ask him what the top three things were that he did not like about the last few events in which he spoke. If it opens up an hour-long complaint session by the speaker, he may be someone you choose not to work with. The answers to these simple questions will tell you a lot very quickly.

One of the most common misconceptions about speaking events is that anyone can simply stand in front of a group and talk. The truth is, public speaking is an acquired skill which can take years to master. There is a lot to consider when speaking to an audience, and you will want to book someone who can keep people engaged, interested, and excited about the information being presented.

More importantly, you need to find someone who understands the purpose of REIA events. While people may attend the event for educational reasons, your group is hosting it to help promote the group, increase membership, and make some money at the same time. An experienced speaker will know exactly how to structure their presentation to achieve this goal. This is a person who has done precisely the same thing countless times in the past.

Someone who has a history of speaking at events like this will also have a more polished presentation. Information needs to be delivered in a certain way. Basic concepts need to be presented before they can be elaborated on. Everything needs to be delivered in a specific order which will build on what was already presented. Your speaker must know how to do this or the audience will end up confused and frustrated.

Focusing on speakers who can prove they are both established and experienced will also help you avoid mistakes. Someone who has a very small following and no real history of successful speaking events may very well cause more trouble than they're worth. I've found there is usually a reason these people are not as successful as others. They may have a bad reputation or are simply not easy to work with. Since the quality of your speaker will reflect on the quality of your group, you need to make a careful decision in this department. The quickest way to find out about someone's reputation is to ask where they've spoken recently. You can find out a lot about a speaker by asking them to reveal the last 5 to 10 places they've spoken. Don't be afraid to ask for phone numbers and contact information of other REIA owners where they have spoken. You may even choose to ask for amount of sales compared to how many people were in the room, amount of returns that took place after the event was over, and any other issues that may have come up.

Unfortunately, this brings up the inevitable cart before the horse. How is a new speaker going to gain experience if no one will give them the chance to get started? Listen, I'm not opposed to taking a chance on a new speaker; however, I would not rely on that speakers' potential income for a particular event to make or break my association. The fact is, unless properly trained, most new speakers are just not going to sell very well. There is the occasional exception; however, it doesn't happen often.

I remember that when I first got started I thought that just by providing enough quality information people would naturally want to buy what I was offering at the end of the evening. I quickly learned that's not how it works. I got a standing ovation my first time speaking. I gave it my all. I taught everything I could teach in 90 minutes. And at the end, I sat there wondering why only three people signed up for my package out of a room of almost 200 people. The truth is, I knew how to teach back then; what I didn't know was how to sell. There is a major difference.

As a matter of fact, it took me a solid three years of speaking regularly before the selling part of speaking really "clicked" for me. There were times when I first got started that I would do pretty well and then go give a similar presentation a few weeks later and not sell anywhere near as much as I did at the previous event. Back then, I had no idea what was working and what wasn't. I was determined to learn, but I couldn't seem to crack the code on what made the biggest differences. Then, finally, about three years or so into it, it clicked for me, and I finally started to not only recognize but understand the secrets behind what makes a presentation worthy of a standing ovation but also sells well. I now teach this strategy at one very small event per year to a handful of other speakers in the industry. As much as I tried to turn this into a science, there is still an art to it as well. That art form comes as a result in part by learning from someone who knows what they're doing, but it also comes from simple practice. In other words, experience.

Obviously, not every speaker will be known throughout the world. Many may be well known locally or will simply have a healthy number of followers. While it can be a great idea to book world-renowned speakers, this simply won't be possible in every case. No matter who your group books, however, they need to be well respected and have a significant presence in the industry.

Are They A Good Match For The Group?

Every speaker will focus on a specific subject, so it's important to make sure they are a good match for the group. Plenty of REIA groups will focus on one particular field in real estate investing. The members will want to hear relevant information which they can use in their own business. Even though a speaker may have interesting things to say, the subject of their presentation still needs to be in line with the objectives of the group.

I was at a "new investor" conference once and saw a speaker totally bomb and sell nothing. Why did he bomb? His subject was on asset protection. The audience didn't have any assets to protect yet; they were all new investors with very little money of their own. Needless to say, the event promoters learned their lesson the hard way. So did the speaker.

When I first started speaking, I was invited by a small REIA to come speak about short sales. Back then I didn't know what questions to ask the association before just saying yes to the opportunity, and I paid the price for it. I showed up to an event that was 99% landlords—all over the age of 60. None of them was interested in my short-term cash producing strategies. Most of the people in the room had decent sized portfolios of free and clear rental properties and were, for the most part, retired. They didn't want to sit and learn a new strategy on how to flip properties; they were more interested in learning how to make their already existing rentals more profitable. Needless to say, that was not a profitable night for the REIA or me, and the poor audience had to sit through a presentation that was of very little interest to them.

It's important to consider the experience level of the group. Some will consist entirely of investors who are new to the real estate market. They may have just purchased their first property and will have a lot to learn. An advanced group, on the other hand, will get bored very quickly if the information being presented is too basic. A speaker needs to be able to address the group on the right experience level. As a speaker who learned this lesson the hard way a few times, I now ask a lot of questions about the group before I will even commit to speak there. This doesn't mean I'm asking these questions to be a jerk or a diva. I really want to make sure the environment is a great fit for both of us. The last thing I want to do is spend time away from family trying to motivate an audience with a subject that is not already motivating to them. The last thing you want to do as a REIA owner is have a speaker come to your association that does not have relevant subject matter.

Location can also be another factor. Some REIA groups will be centered on real estate investing strategies within a certain state or region. Since laws are different for each state, it can be a good idea to find a speaker who has some understanding of local regulations. If your REIA group is focused only on acquiring cash flow rental properties in California, for example, an expert from Idaho may not be the best choice. Of course, this depends on the nature of the subject matter, but you get the idea.

Do They Have Their Own Marketing Plan?

If the speaker has experience, they'll have a marketing plan. And they'll be willing to share it with you.

It amazes me how many speakers don't participate in the marketing of the event. Since it's in my best interest to make sure there are as many tails in the seats as possible, I'm going to do anything and everything I can to help with the marketing process. This means I already have a full-blown marketing process in place that will help implement the effort to fill the seats. Not only am I happy to share it with the promoter, I'm even going to encourage and help with the process to ensure that these marketing items actually get done. We all want to have a successful event, and a speaker should have no problem assisting in this process. If they're not willing to help, there are plenty of other speakers out there that will.

If you'd like to see an example of a proven marketing plan, just shoot us an email to the addresses below. We'll send you a link that provides you with examples of successful direct mail pieces we've used in the past, email templates, voice blast templates, newspaper ads, custom videos, and a whole lot more. Every speaker should have something like this. If they don't, be careful.

To see an example of Larry's marketing plan, please send a request to: **kandas@LarryGoins.com** or call 803-831-0056 and ask for Kandas Broome.

To see an example of Shaun McCloskey's marketing plan, please send a request to: **help@lifeonaire.com**

Simply reference this book in the subject line and let us know what you would like to see and we'll get you everything you need. It will be a whole lot easier for you to see real life examples of this yourself rather than trying to cover it all in one book!

Get References

There is one thing I've found which often separates the good speakers from the bad and that is their willingness to provide references. Every speaker will try to sell themselves to you, but you have to take what they say with a grain of salt. Just because someone claims to be a successful and experienced speaker doesn't make it true.

References are one of the most important determining factors in whether or not to book a particular speaker. The speaker should be both able and willing to provide you with some information about their previous engagements. This can be information about attendance and sales as well as contact information for the people who ran these events.

It may take a little effort but calling up these references will help ensure you're making a wise decision. Many of the people you'll talk to will also be REIA group leaders and will be able to give you an honest assessment of the speaker. They have hosted exactly the same type of event and can give you an idea about how well it went.

If you contact a speaker and they refuse to give you any references, that is a warning sign. Successful speakers are always willing to talk about their past events and will understand the need for references. Someone who doesn't provide this information is probably hiding something and will likely get bad reviews from the people who hosted these past events.

I (Shaun McCloskey) was recently asked to be a keynote speaker at a National REIA Conference where there were approximately 150 REIA owners from all over the country present. They asked me to come and speak about much of what you're reading in this book (How to run a Profitable REIA from a Speakers Perspective). As a speaker, I was not allowed to attend the session they had immediately before I went on stage. That session was called, "The Good, the Bad, and the Ugly." It was a closed room session where each of the REIA owners from around the country were given full permission to openly discuss all of the good, bad, and ugly about any speaker they had speak at their group that year. From what I heard, no one held back. Some speakers were bashed for not having marketing materials at all. Some were bashed for having very low sales. Some were praised for speaking on relevant subjects that riveted the audience and kept them glued to their seats. Others were praised because they gave away great free content to the REIA and really promoted and encouraged the people in the room to become members. Others were praised for knocking it out of the park with sales. The bottom line is, both good and bad news travels fast in this industry, so don't be afraid to ask for references.

Keep in mind, as a speaker, I'm going to do the exact same thing. While the REIA association presidents and owners were in their room having a "Good, Bad, and Ugly" party, myself and a handful of other speakers got our own room and did a little "Good, Bad, and

Ugly" event of our own—all centered around REIA clubs! Some REIAs were praised for having their act together and running a well-oiled machine with great attendance and a motivated audience. Others were critiqued for padding their attendance numbers, running meetings in the back of smoky bars, and more.

Keep in mind, these discussions were not held to be mean-spirited or vengeful. The goal in sharing this information is to inform other groups and speakers of what to be on the lookout for, who needs help with what, who lied about their sales or their attendance, and what to do about it going forward. News travels fast in this industry, and reputation is important from both ends of the spectrum. But it's not just news that travels fast, truth travels faster. The bottom line? Ask for references and then check on them!

Do They Have Good Customer Support

A good speaker should add to your group and not create more work for you. Not only should they already have their own products, they need to have adequate customer support as well. If someone buys a piece of software from your speaker, for example, you don't want them calling your association if they have a problem. Not only will you not have the time to handle it, you might not be able to answer their questions at all.

It's important to remember some products may not be physically present at the event. With the rise in popularity of digital media, many people are turning to things such as ebooks, video courses, and websites as a vehicle for product creation. This can add a unique set of problems when it comes to customer support. If someone purchases access to an online product, they may not run into any problems until they get home.

Customer support becomes even more important in a case like this. The customer is dealing with your speaker's website, files or system, and you simply won't know how it works. More importantly, you have no control over the speaker's system, and you wouldn't be able to help even if you knew how.

The last thing you want is to have a speaker swoop in, unload a lot of products and then disappear into the night. Your group members trust you and will believe you have endorsed everything being sold. If the customers can't get support for the products they've bought, they will feel swindled. Your speaker needs to be able to back up their products with their own customer support network and be able to quickly handle any problems which may arise.

Also, keep in mind that some speakers will have a combination of both digital and physical products as well. Any time a speaker delivers any part of his product digitally, it's vitally important that the REIA hosting the event provides the speaker with a detailed list of all purchasers immediately after the event takes place. This is crucial in order to deliver the digital product quickly and minimize returns. I once spoke at a large event (put on by a very reputable organization) where I sold more than $100,000 worth of products during a 90-minute presentation. Because of the nature of this event, the promoter asked that I deliver a portion of my product digitally so that people wouldn't have to carry a huge bag of product around with them. The event was held at a vacation spot, and it was thought that having to carry around a bunch of product would have been a deterrent for buyers. After countless attempts and phone calls to the promoter, it was like pulling teeth to get the list of people who had purchased product. It ended up taking the promoter close to three weeks to get me a list of all of the customers. Keep in mind, this consisted of more than 100 people that paid $997 for a product that was to be delivered electronically. Not only did the customers not receive a single welcome email for three weeks after the event, they also didn't receive their product. To this day, I still don't know why it was so difficult to get me this pertinent list, but we ended up spending a lot of time on the phone with angry customers, people who felt cheated, people who were asking for their money back. We were able to salvage a lot of the return requests, but it took a lot of hard work, a lot of unnecessary lengthy phone calls, and giving away a lot of additional free materials just to try to save the sale. All of this could have been avoided if we had simply received the list of buyers and their email addresses the same day as the event.

So how can you ensure that the speaker gets this vital information immediately? It's simple. Use 3-part order forms at your REIA. Then, when a customer buys a product, you can give them the pink copy as a receipt, the speaker takes the yellow copy, and the REIA keeps the top white copy. Easy! Now you can get everyone everything they need the same day the event takes place.

Can They Close The Sale?

Education is wonderful, but the truth is, sales are what keep a group alive. As we've already discussed, speaking events aren't solely about making money—we need to provide overwhelming value to our members as well—but profit is always an important concern. A speaker will essentially be a guest sales person who will not only help bring in a large audience but can get them to purchase products as well.

When a REIA group books a speaker, they will generally not pay the speaker a flat fee. The speakers make their money by selling the courses, books, videos, and services they offer. The whole event, in fact, is leading up to this period of sales (typically at the end of the presentation).

Over the years I've learned sales is a skill that not everyone possesses. Someone may be able to give a great presentation and offer a lot of information, but they simply don't know how to close a sale. Because moving products is one of the main reasons for the event, the ability to sell is one of the most important factors in choosing a speaker.

The best way to find out if a speaker is also a good sales person (aside from checking their references and hearing from others) is to simply ask them to provide you with their recent sales. How many people were in the room at the last event they headlined? How many people bought their product? At what price point? It can be far too easy to neglect this piece of the puzzle, so always ask about sales.

Speaking events are sales opportunities; therefore, the products that a speaker offers must be taken into consideration as well. Most people don't realize that public speaking is a business in and of itself. Having a good product requires a lot more than just being able to give a presentation. It requires the materials be presented in a way that is digestible and not overwhelming to the student. It requires incredible customer service, follow up, the delivery of outstanding events, and much more. The challenge is that many speakers may have excellent products and can teach very well, yet they have no idea how to sell from the front of the room. There is a big difference between someone giving a speech that gets a standing ovation vs. giving a speech that is designed to get people to run to the back of the room ready to hand you their money. Most experienced speakers will have made a business out of public speaking. When they work an event, the good ones are going to both educate the audience and sell their own products at the same time. They should be able to do both.

I recently spent a full day with a well-known national speaker who has a history of giving excellent presentations and selling nothing. He came to me upset about the fact that he always gets the standing ovation, that people love to hear him speak, and yet he very rarely sells much (if anything at all). After spending this time with him teaching him how to craft his presentation with the art of selling in mind, he was able to go out to his very next speaking engagement and sell 30 of his products to a room of only about 120 people—and a price point of $797. Truthfully, he could have charged $1497 for the same thing and would have sold just as well. Before this, however, he didn't understand that a selling presentation is not the same as the standing ovation presentation. You can do both, but many speakers don't know how to.

But being able to sell well isn't enough. The products which the speakers sell need to be good. A speaker may be an incredibly gifted sales person and can drive the entire audience to the product table, but if those products are garbage, it can be a disaster. Returns will pile up, your in-box will fill with complaints, and you'll likely lose members. There is nothing worse than having a great-selling speaker come to speak at your event, sell a ton of product, and then end up having a 50% or more return rate because he did a great job selling and a horrible job of delivering what was promised.

Also, there are some speakers that sell well, but sell the entire time. This is the kind of speaker that closes 30% of the room to buy his product, but the other 70% of the room is ticked off and feel their time was wasted. If you have too many guys like this in a row at your REIA, that 70% will eventually stop attending. How do you know to identify this type of speaker in advance? Again, check references. They'll tell you the truth.

What You Need From Your Speaker

There are things you're going to need to get from your choice of speaker that are crucial to the success of the event. At this point, I'm going to assume you've already found the perfect candidate for your event, and we'll move on to what you're going to need to make it a success!

This list of requirements is anything but arbitrary and was created through my own experience with both hosting and speaking at REIA events.

As basic as some of these sounds, they are essential. Remember the "Good, the Bad and the Ugly" event I talked about in the last chapter? One of the biggest complaints that REIA owners had about many speakers is their inability to provide the following things in a timely manner. Keep that in mind when you're looking for the right speaker for your event.

We have actually set up a website where you can watch video testimonials from other group leaders about their experience in working with me, as well as see speaking topics, course information and other ways we can make money together, such as hosting webinars, etc. You can check it out at **www.JVwithTGG.com**.

Okay, here is what you need from any speaker.

A Professional Photo

This is possibly the most basic thing you will need from your speaker. The photo should be a high resolution professional and not just a quick snapshot from a cell phone. You will be using this picture when you promote the event both online and in print. In some cases, the person may be so well known that a picture of them is all you really need to generate interest in the event.

A Bio

The speaker you choose needs to have a brief biography about themselves, what they do, and how they got to where they are now. This will have been carefully thought out and designed to help promote the speaker, which means it is a vital part of your own promotional efforts.

The last thing you want is for a speaker to create more work for you. They should be able to provide their own bio and not rely on you to create one for them. A good speaker will have a collection of different promotional material and this should be included in the bio. Some speakers may have more than one bio if they have more than one presentation.

It's imperative that the person running the REIA, as well as the person announcing the speaker from the front of the room, read through and understand the bio before the event. I've attended REIA events in the past where the host stood up and literally read from the bio, word for word. It was as though they had never even heard my name before, and they read straight from the script. It was impersonal, stilted, and didn't instill a sense of approval or familiarity within the group. Not good! More importantly, it came off as exceedingly unprofessional. You should be able to open the event by introducing the speaker in a natural and friendly way. The best way to do this is to read the bio before the event. (More on this later.)

An Introduction

In addition to a bio, we actually have an introduction. This is a great way to give the group leader exactly what you want them to say to introduce you to their group at the meeting. Ours even says, "Stand up." Yes, I said, "Stand up, and give a warm welcome for Larry Goins!" Once again, it is important that the introduction NOT be read. Instead the leader should become familiar with it prior to the night of the meeting.

Promotional Materials

Most of the people you end up booking will have made speaking at events a major part of their business. Rather than sitting around and hoping to be called in to speak, they will actively promote themselves and what they do. They might do this through websites, email lists, and even traditional methods such as postcards and fliers.

A good speaker should have what is essentially a press kit. They should be able to provide you with a number of promotional items which can be used to help build excitement for the event. Some of these items can be given away to members at the regular meetings.

Doing this can be one of the best ways to create interest in an upcoming event.

If you'd like to see an example of a proven marketing plan, just shoot us an email to the addresses below. We'll send you a link that provides you with examples of successful direct mail pieces we've used in the past, email templates, voice blast templates, newspaper ads, custom videos, and a whole lot more. Every speaker should have something like this. If they don't, be careful.

To see an example of Larry's marketing plan, please send a request to: **kandas@LarryGoins.com** or call 803-831-0056 and ask for Kandas Broome.

To see an example of Shaun McCloskey's marketing plan, please send a request to: **help@lifeonaire.com**

Awesome Free Stuff

A great way to build a relationship with an audience before an event and increase attendance and sales is to give away a bunch of free training before the event even takes place. This can be a free book, video, software, or membership to a website or forum. In our promotional materials that we provide to REIAs, we recently started providing a series of free articles and training videos delivered by email prior to the event. This gets the recipient familiar with the speaker in advance and builds excitement for the live event. Again, our job is to provide our members with overwhelming value, and this is one more way to provide it to them at a very low or no cost. We also encourage the members to attend any follow up events (like Saturday one-day workshops) by giving them yet another free gift for signing up for these events. People love free stuff, and it builds rapport before the event even takes place.

People love freebies. It often doesn't matter what it is, they will line up around the corner to get something for free. If the item being given away is also worth money, like a book, for example, the demand is even higher.

A good speaker should also be a good sales person and so they need to understand this fact of life. Giving something away can often lead to greatly increased sales and an improved interest in the material being presented. Your speaker should have at least one product which they are willing to give away, but it should never be their best product. The giveaway should also never be something that will deter the audience from purchasing the end product offer either. For example, I would never give away my free 300-page eBook on how to rehab a house if I'm also selling a rehabbing course at the live event. If I did this, people might hold off on ordering the course until they've had a chance to go through the free book first. Sounds simple, but this one thing done incorrectly will reduce sales.

More importantly, a free giveaway can drive people to the sales table. I've actually done this myself and have seen how effective it can be. What I give away is a copy of one of my books, the same one you can find in bookstores. The only way the audience can get their copy, however, is by stopping at the sales table and picking it up. A free product will get people rushing to the back of the room. When there is excitement built up around the back of the room, sales increase.

Samples Of Their Products

When you let a speaker sell their products to your group, you are putting your own name on what they sell. This means you need to understand what the speaker is selling and be able to determine if the products are any good. A good speaker will be more than willing to give you some free samples so you can gain a better understanding of the products.

In the past, we've often provided online samples of the training materials to REIAs in advance of being officially booked there.

Many REIA owners are investors themselves and get a lot out of going through the materials. The most beneficial intro I can get as a speaker is when the owner or president of the REIA gets up before I go on stage and says, "Guys, I got Shaun's course a few weeks ago and just by implementing two things that I've learned, I've already made an extra $20,000 this month!"

This kind of thing happens, and it is a huge testimonial to attest to what the audience is getting ready to learn.

Understanding the products is important. You need to take some time to familiarize yourself with the different books, videos or courses they may be offering. It is almost a guarantee that you will receive questions about the speaker's products, and you simply must not come off as ignorant. If the audience feels you haven't taken the time to understand the items being sold, they will have a hard time believing your endorsement of them.

Product Information

This should go without saying. You need to get a list of the products which the speaker will be promoting so you know exactly what's being offered. The speaker should be able to provide you with information about prices and any bundles or deals which might be offered.

For example, a speaker may sell a book at one price, a home study course for another price and a multi-day bootcamp for yet another price. The bootcamp may include the home study course and book as a bonus for people who sign up during the event. Many speakers may even have bonus packages that are only included in one package but not another. It's a good idea for you to get these packages in writing ahead of time, and then set some time aside before the speaker goes on stage to make sure the rest of your staff understands the packages as well.

The last thing you want when people run to the back of the room is confusion about what the speaker just offered in their package. For the most part, the audience will know which package they want to purchase; however, sometimes they're going to have questions. While you may not be able to answer every question that comes your way, knowing the basics of the products offered will help you tackle the majority of questions. It will also help you overcome objections so that you can help sell more product. For example, when I offer a bootcamp package from the front of the room, I also include a live Ustream of the event so that students can watch the event from their home computer if they're unable to travel to a live event. Every once in a while I'll have a student that wants to sign up, but they didn't hear me describe how you could attend the event from home and also get a recording of the event later on. This particular customer may go to the back of the room and only sign up for the home study course because of this, and if you and your staff are aware that this is an objection, you can overcome it by simply relaying what the customer may not have been aware of.

Speaking of live events, you're also going to want to know the dates of any future bootcamps and live training events the speaker will be offering. Have a list of those dates handy at the back of the room, as people will often need the dates repeated. The more prepared you are, the better the back table will run, which will equate to more sales and happier members.

We have a sheet in each of our courses called the "Read This First" sheet. It will answer pretty much any question that someone will have at the back table. In fact, I tell the REIA group staff helping with sales that if anyone has any question the typical answer is: "It's on the Read This First sheet." This helps the staff and volunteers that may get questions they do not know the answer to, such as how to register for the bootcamp or what is the guarantee, etc.

Contract

The contract is one of the most important things you need for every single speaking event. There is no way to tell what might go wrong and as Murphy's Law suggests, what can go wrong will go wrong. Experience has proven to me that it is always better to plan ahead and avoid potential miscommunications along the way. The last thing you need to deal with is a speaker showing up claiming that you promised to provide something which you expected them to bring. Since the contract outlines every last detail, you can simply refer back to it. As a binding legal agreement, there is no way they can argue.

The contract will also need to outline any consequences if the speaker fails to follow the agreement. How severe these consequences are will be up to you. Try to avoid the urge to include huge monetary penalties, because it will cause the speaker to think twice about agreeing to it.

If the speaker has been doing this for a while, they may already have a contract they can send to you. As with any contract, make sure to read and understand it before signing.

If your speaker doesn't have a contract then you can either search for one online or reach out to us and we'll get you one (**help@lifeonaire.com** or **Kandas@LarryGoins.com**). Most REIA groups are well networked, and many of them will share what they use with you, or of course a lawyer can write one up for you. No matter what you choose to do, however, never book a speaker without having something in writing so that both parties know what they're agreeing to.

Some of the most important aspects of a contract are:

1. Date, location, and time of the event.

2. Product specifics

- What is being offered for sale at the event? (product details and price points).
- When and where to ship product offered for sale.
- What will happen with any leftover product that is not sold at the event? (Who's responsible for shipping extra product back? How is this going to be handled?)

3. Division and payment of proceeds.

- (Who is processing the payments? Whose order forms are being used? How is the division of sales handled?)

This is important to decide up front. Many REIAs will want to handle running the payments on their own. I've also spoken at some REIAs that don't have the ability to run credit card payments and have asked me to do so. I'm fine with either way, but it needs to be agreed upon up front so that we can all prepare accordingly. I learned this lesson the hard way one time years ago. I spoke at a REIA event, gave what I felt like was a great presentation, and then finished my close by driving everyone to the back of the room. I actually sold better than usual and there was a ton of people ready to sign up! Just then, the REIA owner said, "Where are your order forms?" The contract that we both signed said that he would be collecting and processing payment, but it didn't say anything about who was to provide the order forms. We both made some incorrect assumptions. I assumed that since he was collecting, naturally he would want to use his own order forms. He assumed—since he'd never had a national speaker to his REIA before—that I would have wanted to use my own order forms with my own return policy, etc... Neither one of us was wrong. Neither one of us knew.

On a side note, whoever is collecting and processing payment needs to be the one to provide order forms. The reason for this is because the order form must show how the charge will show up on their credit card statement. If the buyer fills out an order form that says "ABC REIA" is collecting payment and the charge shows up as

"Lifeonaire or The Goins Group, LLC" on their credit card or bank statement, they may not know what it is and instantly request a charge back for amount of the charge. This looks really bad on your merchant account record, so you want to avoid this at all cost. Instead, make sure that the charge shows up from the same company that the order form dictates. (By the way, if the customer issues a charge back and the charge comes from a different place than the contract says, you'll lose the chargeback dispute every single time!)

4. What is the return policy for products and how will returns be handled?

- Do they get shipped back to the speaker? At who's expense?
- Is there a restocking fee to the customer?
- How long of a return policy are you going to allow? Some REIAs may have a 30-day return policy, while the speaker has a 10-day return policy.
- What happens if someone wants to return the product after 17 days then?

5. Who is providing the audio/visual needs for the event? What will or will not be provided?

We'll talk more about audio/video requirements later, but this is important!

6. How the sales are going to be split?

Most speakers will not expect a flat payment for their presentation but will collect a portion of the sales generated by it. This is not, however, a universal law, and you need to be clear on how the payment will be handled. One of the most common problems for businesses of all types is a lack of communication when it comes to payment. Don't be afraid to discuss this topic as thoroughly as you feel necessary.

There is no "right way" to figure out splits, however, it needs to be determined up front. A pretty typical split is one where there will be a 50/50 profit split on product sales, a 70/30 split on bootcamp sales (70% going to the speaker, 30% going to the REIA, since there are typically more expenses involved in a speaker offering a bootcamp). Oftentimes these splits will take place after credit card fees of 3% are taken into consideration, along with a $1,000 travel allowance for the speaker. Keep in mind that these can vary drastically depending on the demand of the speaker and the size of the REIA group. For example, a more well-known speaker may not even travel to a REIA group that has less than 150 members in the audience; however, he may consider speaking there with a more advantageous split.

7. How many people are going to be in the room? What happens if there are less people than promised?

This is similar to what we discussed earlier. I've been to a REIA in the past where the association president swore they would have at least 100 people at a meeting, only to get there to find a total of twelve people in the room (after he also swore that he implemented my marketing plan). Four of the twelve were his staff members. If there are normally 100 people in the room, I can see having a slow night where maybe only 80 people show up (weather can affect this as well.) But not 12. Many speakers now put clauses in place where the percentage split will vary if the amount of people that were promised aren't in the room. An example of a staggering split may be 70/30 for less than 50 people in the room, 60/40 for 50-75 and 50/50 for more than 75. If a staggered split is used, there also needs to be someone that counts the room for the number of people and verbally tells the speaker just before he goes on stage. This way there is no confusion. You do not normally count volunteers and staff in the room count; you usually count the number of people seated in the audience.

8. What freebie goodies are going to be offered as giveaways?

- A due date for when the speaker is to supply marketing materials to the REIA.
- This is important! Put this in the contact so that you have a way out if the speaker refuses or can't get you what you need in time.

9. What happens if the speaker runs over his allotted time?

This is particularly important in a larger weekend type event where there are multiple speakers. When one speaker goes over his allotted time, he just bumped back every other speaker for the rest of the day. If you get two or three speakers that do this over the course of one day, all of a sudden you have an event that's going on until 10 pm that was supposed to be over at 6 pm. (This does not make the speakers that are scheduled to go on later in the day happy, as you can imagine.) I spoke at an event once where my allotted time was 3:30 to 5 pm. I was to be the last speaker of the day. The speaker that started the day out that morning was to speak from 9 am to 10:30 am. He ended up going until noon, pushing back every speaker for the whole day. By the time I was able to go on stage, it was 7 pm and there were only 17 people left in the room. There should have been more than 200, but the event was announced that it was scheduled to wrap up at 5 pm. People were worn out and they left. Not only was I unhappy that I traveled halfway across the country to speak to only 17 people, the speaker before me was upset as well, and truthfully, so was the audience.

10. Will the association record the event?

If so, the speaker had better know about it and give their approval ahead of time. Some speakers are okay with this, and some are not. I've had some associations want to record me (without my knowledge) and then sell the recording on their website later. Speakers may or may not be opposed to this, but if you're going to record the event, you need to make sure they understand and agree to it.

11. Contact information for all parties.

This is obviously important. But you'll also need backup contact info just in case something happens. I spoke at a REIA once where the REIA owner's phone died before the event, and I had no one else to get in touch with. It all worked out in the end, but it could have been worse if the situation had been an emergency.

12. Blackout periods

This might be a good idea to add to your contract as well. A blackout period simply states that the speaker agrees not to speak anywhere within a certain amount of miles of your REIA within a certain amount of days. A typical example would be that the speaker agrees to not speak anywhere within 90 miles of said REIA within 90 days of this event.

13. What happens if the speaker doesn't show up?

Or worse—what happens if the speaker sends someone else in his place and didn't bother to let you know he was going to do this in advance? (Speaker may not delegate.)

I've seen it happen. If you're booking the speaker himself, make sure it's the speaker himself that will show up unless you've given permission otherwise.

14. Any other promoter obligations and speaker obligations

Anything else that you can think of that may be important. It's best to have it in writing and discussed in advance. For example, if the event consists of two dates (a Thursday night REIA meeting plus a Saturday all-day workshop), you'll want to include who is paying for the room rental for the Saturday workshop; who is collecting payment for the Saturday workshop; how much is being charged; how the split will be taken into consideration...).

Remember to include in your comments that you must get a W-9 form from the speaker if the association is, in fact, collecting payments and then paying the speaker his share later. W-9s are easy to get up front before payouts are completed. They're a lot harder to get at the end of the year once everyone has been paid and gone on their merry way.

Finally, about contracts—keep them simple. We've covered a lot here, but everything we've just discussed can be spelled out in a three- to five-page agreement. Don't make it more difficult than it is. I had one company invite me to speak and then proceeded to send a 36-page agreement. It doesn't have to be so hard.

Book Them

We've now covered the essentials for finding effective speakers for your REIA event. We have attended hundreds of meetings and have collectively spoken at just as many. Over the years, I have seen wonderful events, and I've seen events which fell apart faster than a house of cards. Booking the right speaker is the first element to a successful event, but there is much more to consider.

Once you've found your speaker, you will need to begin planning the event. Everything hinges on your ability to generate interest, promote the event, and get those tails in the seats! Without people in the seats, you will have essentially wasted your time. Worse yet, you will have wasted your speaker's time as well. There's nothing worse that planning for a big event only to have a handful of people show up.

The following chapter will focus on this next step in the process. Promoting your REIA event is just as important as finding the right speaker. Next up, I'll present a number of different methods for increasing the size of your audience as well as honing in on a few methods which I've found to be particularly effective. Using this information, you can generate enough interest and excitement to fill so many seats you may have to set up extra chairs in the room!

Primary Review Checklist For Your Event

This should be your primary checklist for preparing for your event. To have a successful event, you should address all of these issues. Each item listed here will be reviewed in this book.

Preliminary Questions

☐ Why are you booking a speaker?

☐ Do you want someone with general knowledge or niche specific knowledge?

☐ What is the experience level of your group or intended audience?

☐ What are the goals and objectives of your intended audience?

About the Speaker

☐ Is this person well known?

☐ Do they have experience with this sort of speaking event?

☐ Will they understand the purpose of the event?

☐ Are they an expert in one way or another?

☐ Will their presentation fit the needs of the group?

☐ Do they have references from prior events?

☐ Can they provide information such as attendance and sales figures from past events?

The Speaker's Products

☐ Does this person have their own products?

☐ Do they have a customer service network set up to deal with problems and complaints?

☐ Will they provide you with free samples of their products?

☐ Are their products high quality and carry a high-perceived value?

☐ Are they reasonably priced compared to similar products?

What to Get

☐ Do they have a bio?

☐ Have you read through it?

☐ Are you able to introduce the speaker without reading directly from the bio?

☐ Do they have a professional photo?

☐ Do they have their own promotional materials?

☐ Will they be offering anything for free?

☐ Do you have a contract for the speaker to sign?

☐ Do you understand the contract?

Review Checklist for Chapter 3

Your REIA Group's Website

☐ Does your REIA group have a website?

☐ Does it have information about the objectives of the group?

☐ Can someone find out how to attend meeting through your website?

☐ Is there information about the group's leaders?

☐ Does it contain pictures or videos of past events?

☐ Is it regularly updated?

The Opt-In List

☐ Does your website have an opt-in form to collect emails?

☐ Are you offering a good incentive to encourage people to submit their email address?

☐ Are you effectively managing your list?

☐ Do you regularly send useful and educational information to your list?

☐ Are you informing your list of upcoming meetings, events, and product launches?

Social Media

☐ Does your REIA group have a Facebook Fan Page?

☐ Do you have a Twitter account?

☐ Is your group networking through LinkedIn?

☐ Do you post information about meetings and events on MeetUp?

☐ Do you regularly update your social media pages?

☐ Are they linked back to your group's website?

Cellphones

☐ Are you collecting cell phone information from members and attendees?

☐ Have you made submitting cellphone information an enticing prospect for your members and attendees?

☐ Are you using a voice or text blasting service to contact the entire list at once?

☐ Do you use the list to remind people of upcoming meetings and events?

Traditional Promotional Methods

☐ Are you utilizing traditional promotional materials to help promote meetings and events?

☐ Can you expand on this by adding fliers, postcards, magnets or anything else?

☐ Do you have someone distributing fliers around town?

☐ Are you creating things like postcards specifically for a single event?

☐ Are you mailing out this material?

☐ Do you place ads in relevant magazines, newspapers, and newsletters?

Mailings

☐ Are you collecting mailing information from members and attendees?

☐ Have you purchased a mailing list?

☐ Are you working with other local REIA groups to share mailing information?

☐ Have you looked into non-owner occupied properties in the area?

☐ Do you send out coupons, vouchers, and other incentives?

☐ Did you get your speaker to mail their local list?

Review Checklist for Chapter 4

Location

☐ Is the location big enough to accommodate the estimated attendees?

☐ Is there adequate parking?

☐ Are there adequate facilities?

☐ Can it accommodate your technological needs?

☐ Can it handle any catering needs?

Technology: Do you have...

☐ A dedicated A/V person trained in the use of the equipment?

☐ An adequate PA system?

☐ Microphones to meet the needs of your speakers?

☐ A microphone for the audience?

☐ Extra batteries for the microphones?

☐ Extra microphones for back up?

☐ Projectors for either photos or videos?

☐ A simple way to operate the projectors?

☐ A large enough screen for the projectors?

☐ Wires to hook everything up?

☐ Have you tested all of the A/V equipment?

The Sales Table

☐ Do you have a dedicated sales staff?

☐ Are they experienced sales people?

☐ Do they know how to operate the payment processing systems?

☐ Are they familiar with the products and any special offers?

Do you have:

☐ Enough tables to hold all of the products?

☐ A list of all the products you'll be offering?

☐ Order forms?

☐ Pens?

☐ Clipboards?

☐ Stands for displaying products?

☐ A plan for how to organize the products?

☐ Enough products to fill demand?

☐ Promotional items?

☐ A way to collect contact information?

☐ Do you have a way to process credit and debit card payments?

☐ Have you tested this equipment?

☐ Do you have a way to handle cash sales?

☐ Can you handle online sales?

Scheduling

☐ Have you created a schedule for the event?

☐ Are there enough rest periods?

☐ Is the event organized in a cohesive way?

☐ Have you planned for the meal?

☐ Have you planned for distributing the food and collecting the plates?

What you need from the speaker

☐ Have you discussed the equipment expectations?

☐ Do you know exactly what equipment the speaker will need?

☐ Have you discussed the products the speaker will bring?

☐ Do you have all of the order forms or alternative payment methods they will use?

☐ Have you discussed the promotional material?

☐ Are you clear on the payment expectations?

☐ Is all of this outlined in the contract?

What your speaker needs from you

Do they:

- ☐ Understand the experience level of the group?

- ☐ Know the main topic of the event?

- ☐ Understand the local market?

- ☐ Know the estimated size of the audience?

- ☐ Know what the other speakers will talk about?

- ☐ Understand the type of products you'll be offering?

Review Checklist for Chapter 5

Before the Speaker's Session:

- ☐ Have you introduced the group and the topic of the event?

- ☐ Is the audience familiar with everyone who will be on stage?

- ☐ Have you made sure to get everything out of the way before the speaker comes on?

- ☐ Did you leave at least 90 minutes for the speaker's presentation?

Introducing the Speaker:

- ☐ Have you selected who will introduce the speaker?

Are they:

- ☐ Familiar to the group?

- ☐ Respected by the group?

- ☐ Enthusiastic on stage?

☐ Have they memorized the bio/intro?

☐ Have they practiced the introduction?

Sales:

☐ Is your sales staff ready to go as soon as the speaker is finished?

☐ Have you developed a system to keep things moving smoothly?

☐ Does every member of the sales staff understand their job?

Review Checklist for Chapter 6

Updating the Website:

☐ Do you have pictures from the event?

☐ Do you have videos from the event?

☐ Have you posted them on your website?

☐ Are they prominently displayed?

☐ Have you created a brief article which talks about the event?

☐ Have you linked to this article from your social media accounts?

Following Up:

☐ Did you collect contact information from the attendees?

☐ Is your group going to handle the follow up calls?

☐ If so, have you decided who will handle it?

☐ Are they prominent members?

☐ Alternatively, are you going to have your speaker handle the follow-up?

☐ Do they have a team of people who can take care of this?

☐ Do you have information on related products?

☐ Is the person making the calls comfortable with sales?

☐ Can people easily order the new products while on the phone?

Opt-In List

☐ Have you prepared a letter for your email list?

☐ Have you included an affiliate link?

☐ Are you adequately promoting the affiliate products?

The Webinar

☐ Does your speaker have an "Evergreen Webinar"?

☐ Can you offer some sort of incentive, such as free admittance, to encourage people to attend the webinar?

☐ Are you using an affiliate link to send people to the webinar?

☐ Are you promoting the webinar on your opt-in list, website, and social media accounts?

Paying the Speaker

☐ Do you have a set date for payment?

☐ Does this date give you enough time to sort out returns and extra sales?

☐ Will you be ready to pay on the agreed-on date?

☐ Do you have reminders set up to make sure you don't miss that date?

Chapter 3:

How To Fill Your Event With A Die Hard, Hungry Audience—Every Single Time

Finding the right speaker for your event is important, but without an audience they'll be speaking to an empty room. A successful REIA meeting/event can require a good deal of planning. If no one shows up to the event, all the time and effort you put into finding a great speaker will be wasted. This chapter will focus on different ways to promote both your event and your group as a whole. Some of the methods presented may be familiar while others may open your eyes to new ways of building your audience.

A REIA group is only as good as its marketing to get people to the event! You can have the greatest event in the world, but if only two people show up, it's not going to be a whole lot of fun.

So how do you get tails in the seats? First, you need to have the proper exposure, letting enough people know an incredible event is coming up. "We have a meeting coming up," is not a good enough message. You'll need some excellent free content to get people excited about being there. Second, you'll have to prove to people why they should spend (waste?) their time coming.

Now, if you think "waste your time" sounds harsh—good. I meant it to be that way. People won't care about your event unless you give them a reason to care. No one is going to spend his or her valuable time attending an event just because you said so. Remember, time is one of the few non-renewable assets we all have! Once we've spent time on something, we can't get that time back. So your job is to make sure that as many people as possible know about the event, and they need to fully understand why it will be worth their time to attend. It's your job to tell them this, and make sure they really get it. Simple Marketing 101, right? Well, if it's so simple, why do so many REIA associations (and even speakers) mess this up?

Perhaps they've just made it too darned complicated. Let's simplify it a little bit here.

Oh, and one more thing... The speaker can share in this process as well. All of the weight doesn't have to fall on the REIA.

Building Your Mailing List

Before you can begin sending things through snail mail, email, etc..., you'll need to have a list of people to send things to. Just as with your group's opt-in list, you should concentrate on building every aspect of your list, not just your email lists.

Think about it... emails are great, but if all you have is an email list, you may be missing the boat. Some people these days change their email address with same frequency as their underwear. (Okay, I hope you change your underwear a little more often than your email address, but you get the point...) Email addresses change. They certainly change more than physical addresses. Why not get both?

While you're at it, why not get a home and cell phone number (do people still have home phone numbers anymore?), their birthday, and anything else you can use to stay in front of them regularly?

There are lots of ways to build your subscriber base. This chapter will cover many of these in detail.

Other REIA Groups

Okay, this may freak out some of the "scarcity mentality" people out there, but there are probably other REIA groups in your area. While many of you look at these other groups as fierce competition, keep in mind that there's power in working together. Many of your members are going to find out about and attend other REIA meetings anyway; why not work together and decide up front that the way you're going to be outstanding in your market is to be the best REIA in the area! You can do this by remembering that the key to being the best is to provide the most value to your members—not in spending your valuable time worrying about your competition stealing what you've got.

If there are other REIAs in your area, chances are, they're also doing some of the same marketing you're doing to build their REIA. They may also be doing some different things as well. Some of what you're doing is better than what they're doing, and some of what they're doing is better than what you're doing. Why not join forces and benefit from each other in a big way? Contacting these other groups and offering to trade mailing lists and contact information is a great way to quickly double or triple the length of your list. Since all of these people were at one time interested in a different REIA group, they will be a targeted audience with a specific interest in real estate investing.

One way this works really well is if the two competing groups have slightly different focuses. For example, my REIA here in St. Louis (called Lifeonaire REIA) is in the process of joining forces with another REIA here in the area called "South Side REIA." The owner of the South Side is a friend of mine that owns a real estate brokerage. One of the reasons he started the REIA is because he wants to be the go-to broker in the St. Louis area for real estate investors. The REIA for him is a means to build his other brokerage business. He provides great info through the REIA to drive people to the meetings, knowing that, as the owner of the REIA, he instantly receives credibility as the expert in the room. This means that a certain percentage of his members will end up wanting to use the services he offers through his brokerage. He also knows he'll pick up additional real estate agents (who are also investors) to hang their license with his brokerage. Granted, he also profits from the REIA directly by having speakers come every few months and offer products, but the REIA in and of itself is a means to build his other business.

My REIA, Lifeonaire REIA, has a purpose as well. We provide the best real estate education on the planet because our goal with the REIA is to lend money to real estate investors for their deals. We want to become the top lender in St. Louis and put millions of dollars out on the streets. The way we figure it, since lending is our ultimate goal, we work hard to provide excellent education, knowing that the more we teach people how to find and do deals, the more they'll go out and do the deals. Then, a certain percentage of those members out doing deals are going to need money for the deals we taught them how to find. We know that not everyone is going to need our hard money loans, but we also know it's a numbers game and many people will need our services. We provide the most incredible training through the REIA, and we get what we want in return. Granted, we'll also have national speakers at our meetings four times per year, and that will be very profitable, but it's also not the only reason we started the REIA. For us to work with a competitor in our area is without a doubt a win-win.

So how do we help each other? Simple. I tell people at our REIA that we're not the only game in town and that they can benefit from also attending our competitors REIA meetings. The owner of South Side REIA (our competitor) has no problem with this because he knows he's going to get clients out of it to accomplish his goals with the brokerage. He then in turn sends his REIA members to my REIA as well, knowing that I have no desire to compete with his brokerage—I want to lend money. It's a win-win all over again!

For those of you with the scarcity mentality, please listen carefully. Get over it for a minute and trust me on this one. Give it a try! You'll be surprised at how much you can benefit from this approach. And if you're worried about competition, you're probably under the delusion that your members are never going to find out about "that other group." Do you really think that's how it works? That's kind of like not having the talk with your kids about how bad drugs are for them, hoping that if you don't bring it up, they'll never be exposed to the drugs, so they'll never have to deal with it. You and I both know that's not how it works. Your kids are going to find out about drugs one way or another. You might as well be the one that teaches them about the dangers rather than letting someone else teach them.

Yes, maybe that's a harsh example, but you get the idea.

Non-Owner Occupied Properties

There are real estate investors in nearly every town and city in the country. These people will own a number of properties but will likely only live in one. When you find a non-owner occupied property you can be fairly certain you've found someone's investment property. These people are perfect candidates for event promotion, and a list of people who own these types of properties can be a great resource for traditional mailings.

So how do you find these people?

Well, the process can change depending on what area of the country you live in, but I'll give you a few ideas on some things you can do to build up a list of non-owner occupied property owners.

- **Find a real estate agent and ask them to pull you a list.**

Many times, Realtors can search the MLS (Multiple Listing Service) or Realist and do a search for non-owner occupied properties. They can usually search by geographical area so that you can narrow down your list of property owners within the state your REIA operates. This is by far the easiest way to get a list. You could provide the agent with a free membership to your REIA for providing this kind of information. Or, just give them some exposure from the front of the room at one of your meetings and turn their search for you into a little training session about "How To

Get a Realtor To Work For You For Free." If exposure would help them get what they want, you just got a Realtor to do some work for you for free, since you were able to provide value back to them.

Here's how they find the right people: Tell them to search for properties in your desired area where the mailing address on the tax records is different from the physical address of the property. It's that simple.

● **Purchase a Mailing List from a List Provider**

Mailing lists such as these are valuable commodities, and there are a number of businesses who collect, organize, and sell this type of information. Simply buying a list of addresses is the easiest and fastest way to develop a huge collection of different people to market to. These lists will often be organized by interest, as well as a number of other factors, so you'll be able to purchase one relevant to your needs. Not only can you find information about non-owner occupied properties through list providing services like this, you can buy just about any kind of list you can dream up. You can even narrow down the list by how much money people make, whether or not they're married and much more. Companies such as www.listSource.com, www.melissadata.com and Dunn & Bradstreet are a few resources I've used in the past.

● **Title Company**

Some title companies will pull this information for you for free if you're either closing deals with them or they're a sponsor of your REIA. Even if they're not a sponsor, many of them will pull this data for you for a small fee.

● **Your County website**

This is by far the cheapest way to find a list. It may or may not be available in your area; every county is different. Some counties have very up to date websites and some counties don't even have a website. Try it though—it just may give you everything you need.

National REIA Website

If your group is not already a member of National REIA, as a local chapter this should be the first thing you do. National REIA has many ways to help you grow your group as well as many different member benefits, such as discounts on building materials, website sources for you to use, rebate programs at businesses like Home Depot, annual events and cruises, PHP educational programs and much more. To learn more just go to **www.NationalREIA.com**.

Your Group's Website

In my experience, a REIA group's website is one of the most commonly overlooked promotional resources available. Many groups will have a very basic website which contains a small amount of information about the group. The problem is this website can be doing so much more. A group's website is their primary promotional tool, and far too many groups have neglected to promote themselves in this department.

Before you even begin promoting an event, you need to promote the REIA group itself. The best way to do this is with a professional and modern website which is designed to attract a fair amount of relevant visitors. The key word here is "relevant." People who visit your group's site need to be interested in the information the group covers. There are plenty of different places to buy bulk website traffic but most of this is garbage. You need real people that are looking for a group like yours.

Real people expect a certain level of professionalism from a website like this. They will expect it to have a professional look and to be informative and laid out well. People will visit a REIA group's website because they're interested in learning more about the group. They'll want to have a good amount of their questions answered before they even think about attending a meeting or participating in an event. Think of it a little like dating. You want to give out enough information to keep people interested, intrigued, and provide them with everything they need to create a strong desire within them to attend an event. You don't give out every single detail about who you are on a first date (or a dating website for that matter.) Instead, you give enough quality information to peak their interest without giving so much information that it becomes either overwhelming or undesirable for the reader to actually attend a meeting.

A Few Things Your Website Should Include:

• Information about the Group

This could be a simple "About Us" page; it needs to contain information about the purpose of the group as well as the specific focus of that particular group. Since some local REIA groups may have a couple of sub-groups with an even more specific focus, it can be a good idea to link to these and include a separate website or web page for each sub-group. Remember, you want to provide good information without providing so much that it becomes confusing to the visitor.

When you're writing the content for the site, remember to keep the information relevant. Any time I'm writing content for anything, whether it be a website or a book like this, I'm constantly trying to answer the question, "Who cares about this?" If the answer is "no one," it probably shouldn't make its way into the content I'm writing.

• Info about Group Leaders

Your website should contain some information about the leaders of the group. This can be a short bio for each leader with a picture attached to it that explains some of their qualifications. Perhaps your group leaders were highly successful investors who have written books and taught seminars. The experience level of the leaders will reflect back on the group itself. Have some fun with this! People want to attend a REIA that has a fun environment. It is possible to have a fun and professional environment at the same time!

• Pictures of Past Meetings and Events

People relate to images very quickly. One of the best things to include on your group's website is photos of past meetings and events. These need to be as professional as possible and should show off both the size of the group and how much fun the events can be. The best pictures are the ones taken during networking time when people are smiling, laughing, having a great time together. Pictures are one of the reasons Facebook became so popular. People love to look into the lives of other people, and we all know a picture is worth a thousand words. Make sure your pictures say "FUN!"

• Up To Date Info on Future Meetings and Events

While it's not necessary to have the next five years planned out in advance and listed out on your website, people do want to have something to look forward to. I say give them a reason to get excited! Show them a sneak peak of what's coming.

One thing you do not want to do is plan too far ahead. For example, if you're having a national speaker at next month's meeting, it's usually best to focus in on that one event. I've seen REIAs show every meeting and national speaker they plan on having for the next 12 months on their website, and I actually think it could detract from sales at the meeting at hand.

People will often come to your group's website because they are interested in networking with other real estate investors (again, this is where a few pictures say a lot). If the website has done its job, the people that attend the meetings only for networking will also want to attend for many other reasons as well. The key here is to keep the information on the website up to date and relevant so there is no confusion. No one is going to come to this month's meeting if they visit your site and there's been no new updates or content added for the past four months.

• Promoting the Site/Event

Once you've created a professional and enticing website for your REIA group, you will need to get people to visit it. Driving traffic to a website can be difficult if there is no reason for people to visit. There are a number of different ways you can do it; however, one of the best methods is to make use of social media. Over the past few years, social media has exploded in popularity, and these sites can be a wonderful way to tap into millions of active internet users.

On top of this, changes to the way search engines such as Google rank different websites have made social media even more important. To put it simply, every reference to a website is given a certain value. When someone mentions your REIAs website on a social media site like Twitter, Facebook, or even another website blog, your site will receive a certain number of points, which help it reach the top of search engine results. Social media references are now more highly valued than ever, and having a significant presence on these sites will be a great benefit to your group's own website.

• Facebook

Facebook is easily one of the most popular sites ever created, and you simply can't afford to neglect it. There are some people who don't know the first thing about computers, yet they know how to use Facebook. Every REIA group needs to have a Facebook Fan Page that is regularly updated. Keeping it updated is easy. Simply make a note that every time something on the website is updated, the Facebook page is simultaneously updated with the same information. (Note: In some cases a good website developer will be able set this up to update your Facebook page automatically so that it's not a manual process.) Your group's Facebook page should also link back to the group's own website and vice versa. Doing this will allow people to follow your group as well as promote it to their friends and relatives. When you've planned an event, Facebook can also be a great way to continue promoting it. I don't want to turn this book into a Facebook marketing manual (there are plenty of resources out there to help you hone in on this subject), but the fact is, Facebook is a great tool for expanding your reach and should be one of the very first tools you utilize to market your organization.

• Twitter

Twitter is another popular social media site, but the objective is different. Every message on Twitter has a limit of 150 letters or less, making them very short. This is part of Twitter's appeal and it makes it so people check their Twitter feed on a regular basis. Your REIA group should have a Twitter site, which can be used to both promote events and meetings as well as the group's website.

• LinkedIn

LinkedIn is a social media site designed for professionals from all walks of life. While Facebook may focus on the casual aspects of life, LinkedIn was designed to help business professionals network with each other. This makes LinkedIn incredibly important for a REIA group because it could be the best place to find different investors and real estate professionals. Not only can you find new group members, you may even be able to find speakers on this site.

• Meetup

Www.MeetUp.com is a site designed specifically for finding groups and "meeting up." It can be the perfect place to host information about a particular group as well as details of future meetings. These groups can cover any conceivable topic, and many of them are business related. MeetUp can, in fact, be an incredible resource because people will turn to it when looking for events to attend.

Some REIAs that I know run their entire association through meetup.com and don't even have a website of their own, proving how affective this tool can be! There are a few benefits to this site and a few things to look out for as well.

One great feature of MeetUp.com is a setting where you can allow all of your members to email each other as a group directly through the site. The members love this feature and can choose to opt out of these group emails if they prefer. I spoke to one investor last week that loves this feature so much, this alone is one of biggest reasons he's so loyal to his local REIA. He can create a message as quickly as it takes to login to the site and send it, and find out from a huge list of other investors information like who is the best plumber in his area, where to go to get siding, and more. He simply sends an email and it instantly goes to the 1,700 people that have signed up to be on this particular REIA's MeetUp list.

This instant access can be a great thing if you're a member of the group and want quick information or have a property to wholesale. It can be a bad thing in the sense that I haven't yet found a way to filter these messages before they go out to the entire group. This means that some people may take advantage of spamming the rest of the group with non-approved advertisements about their businesses. I heard of a REIA complaining recently because one unknown title company owner became a member of their REIA on MeetUp.com and instantly started sending messages promoting his title company through the group email list. The problem was, the REIA already had a different title company as a paid sponsor to the group, and they didn't like it that another title company—which hadn't paid a dime to be a sponsor—was being exposed to the same people.

Okay, I get that this isn't the end of the world, but I've also heard of another REIA group starting in a city, going to the existing REIA groups MeetUp site and emailing the entire list with a few clicks, letting 2,000+ people know about their new group they're starting. Yes, it happens. The nerve of some people...

While I might sound like I'm contradicting myself with what I said earlier about welcoming cross promoting with other REIA groups, someone stealing my list by having unlimited access to it for free is different than me sharing it voluntarily and getting something in return.

I also heard of a situation where a REIA owner recently got behind on paying his account with MeetUp. Granted, it was by accident—his card had expired, and he no longer used the email address that he had when he signed up with the group, so he wasn't getting the notifications saying he needed to update his credit card info. When MeetUp didn't get payment, they called some of the other competing groups in his area and basically offered up his group to his competition—all for the low, low price of taking over the monthly payment. Needless to say, this was a HUGE problem, since the owner in this case ran his entire REIA through MeetUp. Overnight, because of one mistake, his entire REIA business was gone. The good news is that he was able to call up the other REIA owner that took over his group and they settled on an undisclosed amount to get his MeetUp group back. Even still, it came with a price, and I don't want to run my entire business through something that I have absolutely no control over.

It may sound like I'm bashing www.MeetUp.com. I'm not. It's an invaluable tool, and I believe every REIA should make it a part of their marketing, as it will get tails in the seats and draw people. Just be careful and know what you're getting yourself into.

• The Opt-In List

Promoting your group through websites and social media is important, but this section is about promoting specific events. With that in mind, there is one incredibly useful thing your group's website can do. When you promote an event through social media, you are essentially sending the message out into the world and hoping it will reach people who are interested. Utilizing what's known as an "Opt-In Form" will give your website the power to build a list of specific people who you can keep in contact with.

You've likely encountered an opt-in form before. This is a simple little form which requires you to enter your email address before you can access certain information. Many of these will have a multi-step verification process. This basically means someone will receive a confirmation email and need to click a link to confirm their subscription to the list. This is called a "double opt-in," meaning the person opting in asked for the information, then verified that yes, this is in fact them and not a spammer just entering random email addresses into a web page.

An opt-in list is a collection of different emails which users have submitted. It is essentially a subscription list for a newsletter that gives you permission to send out regular emails to these people. What makes a list like this so powerful is that it is generally made up of people who are already interested in the information your group covers. These are targeted people who have stated their desire to be kept up to date about promotions, meetings, and events. What better person to market to than the person who asked for the information?

All of the promotion you do for the website is designed to drive visitors to it. While the information on the site is important, the real goal is to take the visitors to the next step of your process. You want them to join your list. If you've done this right, you'll begin to collect a vast amount of email addresses. This list is one of the most powerful and valuable promotional tools your group will ever have. If there was one rule I would suggest every group follow, it would be to constantly build this list. It's worth a lot of money to you and your organization!

● Give them a Reason

Some websites have managed to create lists containing tens of thousands of email addresses. This may take some time, but it simply will not happen without some sort of incentive. Everyone hates junk mail and they will often be reluctant to give out their email address simply because you've asked for it. The truth is, you need to give them a reason. And it better be a good one.

The best thing to do is offer something in return for their information. Submitting their email address and completing the verification process will give them access to some sort of free resource. This freebie needs to be highly desirable, have huge perceived value, and should otherwise have some real world value attached to it. One useful tactic is to offer something for sale and then give visitors the option to get that item for free in exchange for their email address.

The following are some of the most common opt-in building incentives:

● A Free Book

Free digital copies of a book are one of the most common incentives. Since your REIA group will likely have a number of different products to begin with, it can be a great idea to offer one of them for free. Ebooks are the simplest material to give away because they provide more value than a simple PDF article or text document. The book should be both relevant and desirable. Some people have even created a book specifically for this purpose, and it will have been designed to appeal to a certain group of visitors while leaving enough questions unanswered that they will seek out more information.

So, how do you get your hands on a book to give away for free if you don't have one? Simple—ask someone who's already written a book if they'll contribute to your cause. Let them know that your desire is to build your email list and that everyone that comes to your site is going to get a free copy of the book by opting in. The benefit to the author is that he will automatically get raving fans from countless people who have been introduced to his book (and otherwise likely would never have been exposed to it).

You can also get valuable books to give away absolutely free as well. We recently did a promotion where we gave away a digital copy of the famous book *Think and Grow Rich* by Napoleon Hill. How did we do this, you ask? Did we call up Napoleon and pay to give away copies of his book? Um... no, he died back in 1970. What most people don't know is that copyright law protects content written for a period of 50 years. After that, it's open game to share. Although this book is one of the most popular wealth building books of all time, it's also a classic that was written more than fifty years ago. This means you can literally go download a copy of it on the web and give it away as a bonus for opting into your list. And it's all perfectly legal!

- **Videos**

The popularity of online videos has been steadily rising over the past few years. While some people may prefer a book, others will enjoy the simplicity of sitting back and watching a video. Videos can, in fact, be the perfect option for a group which focuses on people new to real estate investing. The video can cover some basic information and will entice the visitors to seek out more information by joining the group or attending an event.

This is a huge oversight that most REIA owners don't take advantage of, and it's a whole lot simpler than you might think. Video marketing is incredibly effective. In fact, it's my opinion that video marketing is one of the most effective tools in our marketing world today. Of course, the content of the video has to be worth watching. It has to be short enough to grab their attention and keep it. It has to be detailed enough and provide enough value to get the recipient to not only watch the video, but watch it until the end. It doesn't need to be ultra fancy either. Anyone with a camera on their phone or laptop can take quality video and post it to www.youtube.com. The best part is that YouTube videos are free to post. You can even embed them into your own website with a simple copy and paste of an embed code. (If that's too much for you, your web guy can do it for you in about ten seconds.)

Video provides an awesome opportunity for the members of your REIA to get to know your speaker in advance of the event. It's even a great way for you to promote one of your regular events even if there is no national speaker coming. Video works great!

The keys to video are simple:

- Keep them simple.

- Keep them QUICK! No one wants to watch a 45-minute video. If possible, videos should be two minutes or less according to the studies I've read. People will watch a two-minute video. If they see the little timeline at the bottom of the video and it says 14 minutes, they may realize they don't have 14 minutes to spare right now and think, "I'll save this for when I have more time." The problem is, they rarely ever get more time, so the video is never watched. The only exception to this is if you're giving out free training content that's totally relevant to their investment business and the content is considered high value to the recipient.

- Get to the point. No one wants to hear about your dog (unless your group is a dog owners group.)

- No long intros. I see some videos with a 30-second fancy intro, and the whole time I'm thinking, "Get to it or I'm turning this off!"

In my marketing with REIAs, I usually provide anywhere from one to three videos promoting the weekday REIA meeting, detailing why people should attend. Then I'll do one more video that can be emailed out in-between the weekday meeting and the Saturday workshop (if we do a Saturday workshop also, obviously). This video quickly explains the benefits of doing whatever they have to do to be at the Saturday workshop. Sort of like a little teaser on what's to come.

This gives the audience a chance to get to know the speaker in advance. It also provides really good content. We usually provide at least one video to drive people to the monthly meeting and one additional video driving people to the Saturday workshop.

• Mini-Courses

Home study courses are one of the most common products you'll find in this industry. Many people have created their own courses about real estate investing in general as well as specifics, such as finding the money and beginner investing strategies. Most of these courses will be broken up into a number of lessons. Since many of these courses can be sold for hundreds, if not thousands of dollars, offering the potential opt-in subscriber the first few lessons in exchange for an email can help build your opt-in list quickly.

If you don't have a home study course of your own, find someone that has some training materials that you can give away for free. If you need something like this, contact us and we'll be happy to send you some free valuable content you can use. We have free books, CD's, DVD's and more that we will be glad to bring. Why wouldn't we? It's exposure that we may not have gotten otherwise. Win-win! We apologize for the shameless plug... but you can see how easy it is to get really good content for the purposes of creating a compelling opt in-list! I am sure any good speaker would be willing to provide the same.

● Online Content

Many websites will choose to use what is known as a "Content Locker." This is basically a program which restricts access to certain information unless a visitor submits their email address or joins the website. If your group's website hosts a lot of useful information, this can be another method to increase your opt-in list. The content they will access can come in the form of articles, online education or even a message board.

● What to do with it

Building an opt-in list is great and can help make promoting an event much easier, but a huge list does you absolutely no good unless you know what to do with it once you've got it! The biggest mistake I see so often is that people neglect their email list. Many rarely ever send out an email and will only contact their list when they have an event or product launch coming up.

The problem with this approach is that the people on your list are likely receiving a number of emails every day. If you don't keep in regular contact with your list, they start to forget about you. Just as a plant needs to be watered, an opt-in list needs to be cared for. It's important to send out regular updates and provide useful information in the emails. Articles are a great thing to send out, and this should be done a few times a month. You don't even have to write the articles yourself. You can have others do it for you for free.

Here's an example. At Lifeonaire REIA in St. Louis, we just asked one of our local contractors to write up an article explaining the top mistakes landlords make when renovating a rental property. We asked him to do this because during conversation one day, he was complaining about how most investors try to go as cheap as they can possibly go on their rental property renovations and then end up spending twice the money they planned for with the problems that arise from going cheap. In our conversation he said, "I wish I could just get hold of these guys and get their attention for just ten minutes to tell them the main things they can go cheap on and the main things they should never try to go cheap on!" As soon as I heard this, my ears perked up. I simply asked him if he would write up an article explaining some of these issues and told him I would post it to our REIA site and send out an email to everyone with the article. I would also credit him as being the author of the article and redirect people back to him, which would in turn get him more business and begin to make him known as the go-to contractor for our members. He was thrilled, I got a great article out of it, our members of the REIA got some excellent content—everyone wins! Doing this regularly helps keep your group fresh in people's minds. When it comes time to promote an event, more people will take notice because they've enjoyed your emails up to that point.

The other problem I've seen is waiting too long to start promoting an event. You must start promotions early. As soon as you have the speaker, time, and location nailed down, you should start informing your group. At a minimum, start promoting thirty days out from the event date. This will help build excitement while allowing people enough time to plan for attending the event. This is especially important if you're also doing a Saturday workshop. People need time to plan for being gone all day. Some people have jobs they need to rearrange. Some people have kids they need to get babysitters for. You get the idea. Plan ahead and notify early.

While keeping in contact with your list is important, it's also imperative that you don't harass them by sending too much useless information too often. No one wants five emails a day from you, no matter how good your emails are. It can be tempting to constantly send out emails, but this will come across as spam and people will opt out of your email list. The key is to find a happy medium. A few messages a month is all you'll need to keep your list active and interested. As an event draws closer, the frequency of emails can increase, but always make sure to avoid annoying your subscribers.

I've seen some REIAs send out five emails the day of the event in an attempt to really push people to the meeting, and the truth is, it's overkill.

Traditional Promotional Methods

Modern technology is great and it's made our lives easier, but sometimes it's best to do things the old-fashioned way. If you're promoting an event, you'll want to cover as many bases as possible. Sticking only to modern communications technology could mean you're missing out on a huge audience. No matter how good your website is, there will still be people who have never, and will likely never, see it.

Traditional promotional methods should not be discounted or abandoned. Sending out letters, distributing fliers, and placing ads in printed publications are still incredibly effective promotional techniques. Since there is some cost and effort associated with these methods, they will also help lend credibility to both your group and the event. Anyone can send out an email, but it takes a bit of dedication to create and distribute physical items.

Direct Mail

While electronic communications have become the norm, the old-fashioned mailbox is just as popular as ever. In many cases, a large portion of the physical mail someone receives will be promotional items of one sort or another. A lot of this may be junk mail but if it refers to something the person is interested in they will take notice. Despite what some may think, promotional mailings are still one of the most effective ways to spread information. The best part about these items is the low cost associated with having them printed. Generally speaking, the price will only shrink further as you order more copies.

Postcards are one of the best things to send out. They're colorful, eye catching, and will deliver information in a matter of seconds. It is, in fact, rather difficult to look at a postcard and not absorb some of the information printed on it. Since they're designed to be mailed out, the cost is usually quite low, and thousands of them can be mailed out at once. There are plenty of companies who offer bulk-mailing services and some will even print the items as well.

When sending postcards, try to send the biggest size you can afford to send. Postcards that are the same size as monthly bills get lost in the mix. Larger postcards tend to stick out and demand more attention. Although this book isn't designed to be a complete course on how to send direct mail, make absolutely sure your headline stands out. Having a headline like "Don't Forget Our REIA Meeting This Month" is nowhere near as affective as "Student Right Here in St. Louis Cashes in on $75,839 Profit House Flip!"

Coupons and discounts are another great item for the mail. Sending out a voucher offering a discount on products can be a wonderful way to entice people to attend an event. Everyone likes to feel as if they're getting a good deal on something, and these coupons will help nurture that feeling. For specifically targeted individuals, offering free admission is often a very effective way of getting them to come to your event.

Flyers work great too; however, this sort of material needs to be posted in places where people will see it. It can be time consuming to canvas an entire city, posting fliers on light poles and pinning postcards up in coffee shops. One way to speed things up is to simply hire someone to do it for you. There are plenty of people, such as college students, who will do odd jobs to earn some extra cash. Websites such as Craigslist are wonderful places to find these people, and they can be hired for a very affordable price. Some towns even have companies that will canvas entire neighborhoods or business centers for as little as $.03 per flyer. It's often easy to cover a lot of ground for very little cost. Of course, the downside with this approach is that it's not a laser-focused form of marketing, but it does work.

As mentioned previously, you can also get your speaker to mail the local people on their list to invite them to your meeting.

Print Publications

Placing an ad in print publications can be a great way to reach a targeted audience. Since the publication will thrive on building its readership, they will likely have quite a large audience. Most publications will have a specific focus, which means this is a targeted and relevant audience, the perfect type for promoting a REIA event.

The most obvious publications will be related to real estate. There are plenty of different magazines, newspapers, and newsletters that focus solely on real estate and these should be a primary focus. You should also be able to find other publications that cover investing and general business related topics. Most towns or cities will have a local business newspaper that is read by almost every businessperson in the area. This can be a wonderful resource and will allow you to reach people who may be just outside the world of real estate investing.

Text and Voice Messages

Cellular technology has become ubiquitous in our modern world. Not only do people have their cell phones on them at all times, they will generally check every single message they receive. This makes cell phones one of the best promotional resources you can find.

One of the challenges is that collecting cell phone information can often be a bit harder than collecting emails. Many people will be reluctant to hand over their cell phone number in an opt-in form. While they may not mind receiving emails, many won't want to receive text or voice messages from someone they don't know. What this means for you is that collecting this information in person may be the best way to do it.

When you hold regular meetings, have new attendees fill out a new member form which asks for this information. Also, if you don't have this information from your existing members, get it from them as they sign in for the meeting. Sometimes all you have to do is ask for it. Offering an incentive such as regular coupons or discounts is one way which businesses of all types have built their list of cell phone numbers.

Events are an even greater resource for this. Since many of the people attending the event may not yet be members of your group, you'll want to take advantage of this opportunity. Simply make filling out the form a part of the event. You can make it a requirement for purchasing tickets, or, once again, offer some sort of incentive.

Cellphones are arguably even more personal than an email address. While people will check their emails at certain times of the day, they will receive text messages and phone calls 24 hours a day regardless of where they are or what they're doing. This means it can be very easy to annoy someone by constantly sending out messages. I wouldn't send out more than one text per month. Used sparingly, it works great. Used too much, you end up ticking off good members of your group. It's easy to overdo this, so avoid the temptation to send too many text messages. Remember, the purpose is to keep them excited and remind them of the event.

Cell phone information is used for what is known as "Text Blasting" and "Voice Blasting." This list of numbers can get to be quite long, and it would be impossible to send out messages one by one. There are a variety of different services that will allow you to create one message and send it out to the entire group. This can be either a text message or a prerecorded voice message which can be sent to every number on the list with the click of a button. Simply searching Google for "Voice Broadcasting" will reveal a number of different options.

A few services we've used in the past:

www.betwext.com for blasting group text messages.
www.slydial.com is great for blasting out voicemails because it will call cell phone numbers and force the call to go directly to the user's voicemail. What's great about this is that the member's cell phone won't even ring. Instead, a notification will pop up on their phone letting them know they have a voicemail. This way, they're not interrupted but will still get notification of the message.

Promote Early, Promote Often

Now that you understand some of the most effective promotional methods, it's time to get started. Even if you don't yet have an event planned, you should be continually promoting your group and its website. The success of any single event is heavily dependent on your success as a group.

Some of the methods I've presented in this chapter can be utilized right away. Strategies such as creating a Facebook fan page and setting up an opt-in form on your website can be completed by the end of the day. Creating a list of relevant people to whom you can promote your events is all about time. The longer you spend on it, the longer your list will be, so getting started right away is the best strategy.

Remember that some of these techniques will require a minor investment, while some you can do for free. If you're on a budget and don't have the money to implement some of these things, there are a few others you can implement that will cost you little to nothing and require very little work. While some of the methods in this chapter can be implemented immediately, some can, and should be, planned over a period of time. Remember the old saying about how to eat an elephant? The answer is… one bite at a time. Setting all of this up won't happen overnight. Pick two or three things you can begin to implement right now and get started. You can always build the rest as you go.

A good friend of mine who's very successful in real estate and a variety of other businesses once said, "I'd rather not sit in an airplane while it's going down. Instead, I'd rather just jump out of the plane and build my parachute on the way down." While that sounds a little scary, it's worked out pretty well for him. I would encourage you to take the same approach in our marketing plan.

All of the suggestions in this chapter can be used together. A successful promotional campaign will make use of a variety of different methods that all complement each other. These methods work together, each one strengthening the other, until you've created a truly irresistible campaign that has people beating down the doors to your event.

Always keep the big picture in mind and develop a total campaign strategy that targets as many different niches, groups, and individuals as possible. While each one of these methods is helpful, using them together is what makes them truly powerful. Take some time to create a full-featured campaign strategy that not only focuses on an individual event but considers the success of the group and all future events as well. This is the key to hosting one incredibly popular event after another.

Review Checklist For Chapter 3

Your REIA Group's Website

☐ Does your REIA group have a website?

☐ Does it have information about the objectives of the group?

☐ Can someone find out how to attend meeting through your website?

☐ Is there information about the group's leaders?

☐ Does it contain pictures or videos of past events?

☐ Is it regularly updated?

The Opt-In List

☐ Does your website have an opt-in form to collect emails?

☐ Are you offering a good incentive to encourage people to submit their email address?

☐ Are you effectively managing your list?

☐ Do you regularly send useful and educational information to your list?

☐ Are you informing your list of upcoming meetings, events, and product launches?

Social Media

☐ Does your REIA group have a Facebook Fan Page?

☐ Do you have a Twitter account?

☐ Is your group networking through LinkedIn?

☐ Do you post information about meetings and events on MeetUp?

☐ Do you regularly update your social media pages?

☐ Are they linked back to your group's website?

Cellphones

☐ Are you collecting cell phone information from members and attendees?

☐ Have you made submitting cellphone information an enticing prospect for your members and attendees?

☐ Are you using a voice or text blasting service to contact the entire list at once?

☐ Do you use the list to remind people of upcoming meetings and events?

Traditional Promotional Methods

☐ Are you utilizing traditional promotional materials to help promote meetings and events?

☐ Can you expand on this by adding fliers, postcards, magnets or anything else?

☐ Do you have someone distributing fliers around town?

☐ Are you creating things like postcards specifically for a single event?

☐ Are you mailing out this material?

☐ Do you place ads in relevant magazines, newspapers, and newsletters?

Mailings

☐ Are you collecting mailing information from members and attendees?

☐ Have you purchased a mailing list?

☐ Are you working with other local REIA groups to share mailing information?

☐ Have you looked into non-owner occupied properties in the area?

☐ Do you send out coupons, vouchers, and other incentives?

☐ Did you get your speaker to mail their local list?

Chapter 4:

What To Do Before The Event To Virtually Guarantee Success

Every successful speaking event starts long before the speaker shows up. The initial set-up stage is vitally important because you're creating a solid foundation on which to build a productive and enjoyable REIA event. The way you organize everything will contribute just as much to the success of the event as anything the speaker might say. If you neglect anything during this stage you will be setting up your group for failure.

This chapter will focus on what must be done before an event can take place. This is information we've learned from years of real world experience. We've attended events that ran like clockwork and events that could not have gone any worse. We've noticed a few mistakes which seem to be a common occurrence in every unsuccessful event, and this chapter will help you avoid them.

Plan Early, Plan Often

The planning stages of a REIA speaking event will likely account for a lot of the time you spend on it. There are many different things to consider if you want it to run smoothly. Neglecting to plan as thoroughly as possible is a recipe for disaster. I have attended a few events, both as a speaker and an audience member, that were poorly executed. Not only did that group waste a lot of time, they spent money that would have been better used some other way.

You should start planning your event as early as possible. If Murphy's Law has any truth to it at all, there will be a few problems along the way. Giving yourself enough time to handle these problems is the key to hosting a successful event. Meeting with venues, vendors, and speakers will allow you to cover all of your bases and keep everyone on the same page.

If there is one thing I would suggest you never forget, it would be contracts. You simply must have contracts for everyone, from the venue to the sales staff, vendors and the speaker as well. Part of the secret to hosting a successful event is avoiding arguments or problems in communication. Contracts will help protect you in countless ways. I have seen people scoff at the need for contracts until a problem came up. They were able to rely on the strength of the contract to protect themselves and now they insist on it every time.

The Location

The location of the event is the most obvious initial consideration. Before a speaker can come in and talk to your group, you'll need a place for them to do so. There are several things to keep in mind when looking for locations, and these are very important considerations. Finding the proper location is a matter of understanding the needs of the event itself. You'll want to find one which will provide everything you need to keep your audience happy and comfortable.

Size and Capacity

Different events will vary in size. Some may be rather small and will consist mostly of REIA group members. Other events, such as weekend long seminars, will often attract a much larger audience. First and foremost, the event location must be able to host the expected number of attendees. This can be hard to predict, but the amount of promotion and the fame of the speaker can give you an idea.

In addition to this, you'll want to leave room for any unexpected attendees. If your promotional efforts were really powerful, you may find yourself with a far larger audience than you expected. There is nothing worse than needing to scramble around at the last minute, hunting down extra chairs and supplies. Always leave room for people you weren't expecting.

Parking

The availability of adequate parking is another important consideration. If your event is being held in a major city such as New York, many of the attendees may not drive to the event. In most cases, however, parking will be an important thing to keep in mind.

First, you will need to make sure there is enough parking available for the projected number of attendees. This parking should also be as close to the event location as possible. If the location has its own parking then this option is even better. The cost of parking is important as well. As a general rule, parking should be free. The reason for this is that many people are reluctant to pay for parking and will waste time trying to find a spot on the street.

Facilities

An event location will also need adequate facilities. Depending on the length of the event, these facilities will become increasingly important. During a weekend long seminar, people will need to use the bathroom, charge their cellphones, and take periodic breaks. The length of the event and the number of attendees will determine what facilities are needed.

To put it simply, a 500-person event will need far more than one bathroom. These bathrooms need to be well maintained and able to accommodate multiple people at any one time. Many events will have scheduled breaks so people will be using these facilities at the same time. Keep in mind that you will need bathrooms for each gender and stalls that are handicap accessible.

The overall feel and look of the event is also important. I remember when I took over the REIA in St. Louis. One of the first things we changed is the event location. The meetings took place in an Elks Club, which required attendees to walk through a smoke filled bar just to get to the meeting room. Even the people who smoke complained that there was just too much smoke. There's nothing worse than leaving a REIA meeting and having to immediately throw your clothes in the washing machine when you get home and take a shower before going to bed.

Another speaker told me how he once spoke at an event where the meeting room was inside a fitness center. While he was in the middle of his presentation, a few of the younger guys working out in the room next door thought it would be funny to grunt as loud as they possibly could while using the bench press machine. As if that weren't enough of a distraction, eventually the grunts turned into sexual moans that were way out of control. It may have been funny to the two guys in the fitness center, but it was not so good for sales that night.

Technological Considerations

Every event will require a certain level of technology. The audio/visual equipment will need a power source, and you may want to provide power for your attendee's devices as well. Some aspects of an event might require internet access, so it's important to have a secure, reliable, high-speed connection. Most modern locations will also be able to provide wireless internet access, so you will need to understand how their system works.

Catering

Catering will be an important thing to keep in mind for certain events. Shorter events may have some simple refreshments—such as cookies and coffee—that can you can easily handle on your own.

Other events may revolve around a meal, and this will make things a bit more complex.

If you're holding the event in a hotel, the location may be able to provide all of the catering. This will include the storage and preparation of the food as well as its delivery to the attendees. Before you sign anything, always make sure you understand the costs associated with this aspect of the event and factor that into your budget.

The Setup

Once you've nailed down the location of the event, it's time to begin planning it out. The logistics of the event will determine much about the way everything is set up. You'll need to keep all of the requirements in mind while you create your plan. Try to visualize how everything will go. Imagine the event taking place and try to pinpoint any possible problem areas.

The most important aspect of setting up for an event is timing. You'll want to have everything set up and ready to go before the first person walks through the door. I have personally attended events where the hosts were still setting things up as people started to arrive. This gives the impression of being unprepared and will reflect negatively on the group as well as the speaker. People will find it hard to trust your endorsement of the speaker if you've failed to handle the event professionally.

The room

   • **Setting up the Chairs**

The way you set up the chairs may seem deceivingly simple but it can be relatively complicated. Most locations will simply be a large, empty room. You'll need to fill it with seats that are arranged in such a way as to make the best use of the space available. As with every other aspect of setting up your event, the type of event will determine the way the chairs should be organized.

Different events will have different needs. A small group meeting will require a more intimate setting, while a large, weekend long seminar will need much more space. Try to consider the type of atmosphere you want to create. Is it going to be large and impressive or close and personal?

There are three most common ways to arrange the chairs and each one is a bit different:

−Theater Style

Theater style seating will be the most common. This format follows the same basic plan as any movie theater. It's meant to maximize the use of space by allowing the largest number of people to still be able to clearly see and hear the presentation. The reason this is so commonly used is because it can be scaled up or down depending on the number of attendees.

When arranging chairs in a theater style configuration, try to stagger each one. Leave a bit of space between each chair, a few inches should be enough. The next row of chairs should be set up so each one looks out between the two chairs in front of it. This makes it so people will still be able to see the stage even if the row in front of them is filled.

Keep in mind that the stage, with its screen, is the primary focus of the audience. No seat should ever be obstructed and each one should have as good a view as the next. If your event location is very large then you may need to consider a semicircular formation, much like a baseball stadium. This will keep each chair pointed at the stage, allowing each person to see clearly.

−Round Table Style

A round table formation will be quite a bit different from the typical theater style formation. In this arrangement, the chairs will be centered around a number of tables that are dispersed throughout the room. This configuration is most useful for any type of event that will be serving a meal. Because people will already be sitting at a table, it will be much easier for them to eat without the need to move around.

In addition to this, the wait staff will be able to keep track of what each person ordered. The way the tables are set up will also give them plenty of room to move from table to table while carrying trays of food. Since the speed of this portion of the event is important, a round table format can be incredibly useful.

Round table arrangements can also be great for any sort of event that will require people to work in groups. Many speakers include an interactive portion of their presentation. They may, for example, give a list of sample properties and have the audience break up into groups so they can put the lessons to work. Using the round table format for the seating means the audience is already set up in groups, which will help everything move smoothly.

When choosing to use this style, consider the size of the room and the number of attendees. Each table should only hold about six to eight people. This gives everyone plenty of room to eat, set up their computers or just sit comfortably. The stage will still be the main focus for the audience, so the tables should be staggered in a fashion similar to the theater style arrangement. Due to the nature of this seating style, it may be a good idea to assign seats.

−Classroom Style

A classroom style seating arrangement is great for long seminars. An event lasting all weekend will likely present a lot of information. This will be an educational event designed to deliver in-depth information about a particular subject. These events may have worksheets or handouts that people will need to follow. Since there will be so much information to process, the audience will also want to take notes.

This configuration will make use of long tables. Ideally, the audience should only be seated along one side of the table, the side facing the stage. This will let them take notes without the need to look away from the stage. In addition to this, the speaker can address everyone face-to-face rather than having people constantly turn around.

The tables can be set up in rows, rather than staggered. Remember that you want to make it as easy as possible to move between the tables. The best way to do this is to create aisles between each column of tables. You could, for example, break the tables up into three columns with an aisle between each one. This will not only allow people to move around but will foster a stronger classroom feeling.

Regardless of how you set up the room, make sure there are no doors off to the side of the stage. Nothing is more distracting than an attendee walking up in front of the room, right in front of the speaker, to leave the room or go to the bathroom. The best exit is the exit in the rear of the room, away from potentially becoming a distraction. Speaking of distractions, even windows in the room can create distractions. I once spoke at a REIA meeting where there were floor to ceiling windows off to the side of the room. There was a lot of construction going on outside, and I found myself competing for the attention of the room every time the huge bulldozers and Caterpillars drove by.

Audio and Video Equipment

The audio and visual equipment will play a major role in any presentation. Most speakers will have some sort of modern presentation already prepared. This can include videos, slide shows, and even live programs. This aspect of what the speaker does is a vital part of the entire event, and it needs to be a primary focus.

Correctly setting up and calibrating all of the audio/visual equipment can be rather complicated. This is why I always suggest you hire a trained, professional, and dedicated audio/visual person. Some people will see this as an added expense, but it's one that you should not neglect because the quality of the presentation is every bit as important as its content.

In the case of a major event, it can be a good idea to have an entire audio/visual staff. With multiple speakers and different presentations to worry about, there's a good chance things may need to be moved around during the event. Spending a little extra money and hiring an A/V staff will be a major beneficial contribution to the success of the event itself. These people will ensure everything runs smoothly and will free you from the need to worry about it.

While setting up the A/V equipment is important, you'll also want to test the entire system before the event starts. No matter how many times someone may have set up the same exact system, something can still go wrong. Speakers can blow out, wires can fail, and microphone batteries will die. Testing the system will help you avoid any embarrassing problems.

I simply can't stress this aspect enough. I have personally been invited to speak at events where I've shown up, expecting to have everything ready to go. When I got there, however, I realized I would need to figure out how to plug in my computer without any help. I scrambled around, trying to find wires and power sources, as people were taking their seats. This is one of the absolute worst first impressions you can make on your audience and will seriously impact the success of the event.

The amount and type of A/V equipment will vary from event to event but the most common items are:

PA System

A good PA system is a must. Many events will be held in a large room and the people in the back will need to be able to hear the speaker's presentation as clearly as possible. Depending on the size of the room, one or two speakers may not be enough. You need to consider the entire layout of the room and make sure that every seat is covered.

We use a Bose L2 System at our REIA, which works great for a room of up to 400 people. Bose also makes an L1 system that is considerably cheaper. If you're going to handle the audio yourself, both systems are fantastic and have crystal clear audio. You can even plug an iPod or something similar into them to have music playing during breaks. The reason I went with the L2 system is because it takes less than two minutes to set up and it also came with a miniature mixer so that we could plug in up to four microphones. There is also a USB hookup so you can hook the mixer directly into a computer and record the audio from each event. What you get is crystal clear, studio quality audio that can be repurposed later and sold after the event takes place. (Great for creating products you can offer for sale at a later date!)

Another option is investing in something even less expensive like the Fender Passport system. You can usually get one of these for less than $400 and they sound great as well.

It is possible to use the audio systems that come in hotel rooms, but be careful with this. Not all hotels invest in their audio systems, and some are downright terrible. The last thing you need is muffled audio. If the audience has to concentrate just to hear the speaker, sales will suffer. In addition, many hotels charge a ridiculous amount of money to rent their in-house system. In some cases you may be able to own a system of your own for the price of renting a hotels system just once.

In any scenario, make sure you test whatever audio system you choose to use in advance. No one enjoys last minute audio failures or challenges, including your speaker and certainly your audience members.

Microphones

A PA system is worthless without microphones, so you will need to have these on hand as well. The type of microphone you choose is also an important consideration. Some speakers will like to move about the stage, emphasizing their words with pantomimes and sweeping gestures. Small lapel mics and lavalier microphones are the ideal option for this type of person. Some speakers, on the other hand, may stand at a podium and won't want to be wearing a mic. Make sure to talk to your speaker to determine what they would prefer.

The speaker isn't the only one who will be using a microphone. Many events will have a question and answer period, so it's important to have a microphone available for the audience as well. When someone asks a question, you'll want everyone to be able to hear it so the speaker doesn't have to constantly repeat what someone said. This microphone can be set up on a stand or passed around by a staff member.

Remember, also, that many microphones will run on batteries. This is especially true for any sort of wireless microphone. Make sure to check the batteries in each one and keep a few fresh batteries on hand just in case. In addition to extra batteries, you should have a few backup microphones in the event that one of them simply fails for no real reason.

Two recommended brands of microphones are Sennheiser and Shure. Both companies make top-notch microphones that sound great and take a pretty good beating.

Projectors And Screens

Most speakers will have some sort of visual presentation. This can be as simple as a slide show or as complex as a video. You should always talk to your speaker to determine what type of projector they'll need. Make sure it will be compatible with the way they'll deliver the presentation. Some equipment may only work with a PC while others may only work with a Mac. If the speaker will provide a DVD then you'll also need a DVD player which is hooked up to the projector.

You'll also want to provide an efficient way for the speaker to operate the projector. Some people will simply plug their laptop into it and will be able to operate it that way. Other speakers may want to have a remote control which will allow them to change slides or pause and play videos without touching a computer. Make sure they understand how to use this device before the event starts.

Where you place the projector is also an important consideration. You'll want to keep it in a location where it won't interfere with the audience. There may be plenty of wires connected to it and these can be a safety issue if the projector is in the middle of the room. Try not to obstruct the aisle and keep it elevated so no one will block its projection.

The screen will also need to be clearly visible to everyone in the room. This can be somewhat tricky with a circular room set up but try to avoid angling it in any one direction. The speaker will also need to be able to see what's on the screen during the presentation, so keep this in mind.

The Sales Table

Selling products is one of the primary reasons for hosting a REIA speaking event. You should focus just as much attention on the logistics of the sales as you do on the presentation. We will cover the specifics of how to set up the sales tables in the next few pages, but we feel it's important to include some information on what you'll need first. Sales are part of the event, but in a way, it's also a separate entity and approaching it with this mindset can help make things easier.

Just as you'll want to have a trained audio/visual staff on hand, you'll also want to have a trained sales staff. If everything goes well, people wanting to purchase products will surround the sales table. Anyone who has ever been in a retail situation can attest to the fact that this can quickly become chaotic and disorganized. If the sales are handled poorly, you absolutely will lose customers. This is a fact.

The sales table needs to be adequately staffed by people who know what they're doing. The number of attendees can often determine the size of the sales staff. As a general rule, plan for having every single person in the audience at the sales table and hire a staff accordingly. You'll want to have enough people that some can be processing payments while others are handling customer service.

Your sales staff should also be experienced sales people. They need to be enthusiastic about what they're offering and able to transfer that enthusiasm to potential customers. The worst thing you can do is have an apathetic sales staff that could care less about the number of items sold.

They will also need to be familiar with the products so they can effectively answer questions. Some of the products will be familiar while others may be specifically related to the speaker. This is where the product samples become important. Make sure your sales staff has familiarized themselves with each product and understands what they're selling. An effective sales staff will be able to suggest related products and describe any sort of package deals which may be offered.

In addition to the sales staff, you should also have:

• Payment Processing Systems

People will generally pay for products in one of two ways, so you need to accommodate both options. Some people will pay with cash, and a trusted staff member should handle this. You should also consider using a real cash register to help streamline the process. Other people may want to pay with credit or debit cards, so you'll need to have credit card processing machines as well.

Your sales staff needs to be familiar with these machines. The point of sale is an incredibly important time and it can determine whether someone walks away happy or leaves without buying something. Traditional credit card processing machines will need to be hooked into a phone line and you should test this connection before the event. There are also some modern devices that can be plugged directly into a cellphone or tablet. These may be wireless but you should also test the connection before the sales start.

• Order Forms

Some products may need to be ordered and provided at a later date. This can include things such as online products, large digital courses, or one-on-one mentoring. It's important to have enough order forms to fill the demand. If you run out of forms then you will have effectively limited your potential sales, so always have more than you think you'll need.

Since people will be filling these out by hand, you should make sure to have enough pens available. Keep in mind that you want to accommodate as many customers as you can, so I would suggest having a number of clipboards, preloaded with the order form, available to hand out. If people need to huddle around one or two order forms you will likely lose a few customers.

• Product

The most important thing to have is the product you'll be offering. Without products, you'll have nothing to sell. Your REIA group will probably have a collection of different items which you sell at meetings and events. The speaker will also bring products with them. You'll need to know what type of items they'll be offering so you know how to set up the table. We'll cover the specifics of setting up these products later.

• Information Collection

In the previous chapter, we illustrated how important it is to use events as an opportunity to collect information about the attendees. Because the sales happen at the end of the event, this is the perfect time to have them fill out a contact form. Try to keep this separate from the actual sales. It can be a good idea to have them fill out the contact information right after purchasing a product. Since they have already proven their interest in your group's material, they will be more likely to fill out the form.

• Location

The location of the sales table is the first thing to consider. Because it is such an important part of the event, you'll want it to be prominent and accessible. At the same time, however, you don't want it to distract people during the presentations. The best location for the sales table is in the back of the room, right by the exit. This creates a situation where the audience has no choice but to stop by the table, much like the way a museum will place its gift shop next to the exit.

• Shape

In most cases, the sales table will actually be made up of multiple tables. While these can be arranged any way you'd like, I've found the best configuration is a U shape. If you have three tables, for example, one will be in the middle and another will stretch out from each end, perpendicular to the center table.

This shape will create a virtual store. When someone heads over the sales table, products on all sides will basically surround them. No matter where they turn, there will be products on display. This helps to keep their attention captivated on the products and encourages them to stay there rather than wandering away. It will also keep your customers contained to one location, which makes everything easier on your sales staff.

Once people have chosen their products, they'll need to pay for them. You want to make this as quick and easy as possible so they can pay and move on, making room for the next customer. The location of the cashier is an important consideration. A line will quickly form at this spot, which can then begin to crowd the rest of the table. It can be a good idea to either keep the cashier at the end of the table or set up a separate table for it. For larger events, consider having multiple cashiers or using one person for cash and another for credit or debit cards.

• Display

If the sales table is one of the main focuses of any event, the products are the main focus of the sales table. The way you display each product can do a lot to help increase the sales. The key is to find the right balance between displaying plenty of products and crowding the table. Too few products will make the table feel empty while too many products will make it difficult for your customers to make a decision.

It is a good idea to draw up a plan for the way the products will be displayed. Keeping products organized by category can be a great place to start. Your sales table may, for example, consist of products about finance, investing, and property management. Each one has a different focus and may appeal to a different person. Keeping everything separated by category or topic will help people find products they're interested in without the need to hunt them down.

Over the years I've realized there is also a delicate balance to how many copies of each product you should keep on the sales table. People will often want to examine a product before they purchase it. If you only have one copy of the product on display then only one person can check it out at a time. Piling huge stacks of products on the table, however, can quickly lead to a chaotic mess. Keep a few copies of each product on display and the rest of them under the table, within reach.

Your speaker will also bring along a collection of different products. Since the speaker is the main attraction of the event, their products should be prominently displayed. Their entire presentation may, in fact, revolve around the information presented in their products, so the audience will be interested in looking at them. Placing the speaker's products in the center of the sales table will help make sure they are easy to find.

• Traffic

If you want to sell products then you'll need to have people at the sales table. While some people will stop by the sales table anyway, you want to get as many people running over there as you can. This is where a free give-away item can be incredibly powerful. I've personally used a free promotional item to successfully send the entire audience over to the sales table where they can't help but look at other products.

When I'm invited to speak at an event, I will always bring a stack of CDs that I plan on giving away for free. Towards the end of my presentation I'll hold up the CD, tell the audience what it is, and then mention that it's entirely free. I'll generally have a couple of copies with me while I'm on stage. A few people will then run up to the stage to get their own copy. Now that the audience has seen the demand for this product, I mention how there are plenty more over at the sales table. As I've said before, everyone loves getting something for free and it's rare that people don't rush over to the sales table to pick up their copy.

A Schedule of Events

If you've ever been to the theater then you'll be familiar with the Playbill. This is a small pamphlet describing a bit about the show and the people acting in it. More importantly for us, however, it also gives the audience a general idea of how the show will be scheduled. It tells them what acts come first, when the intermissions are, and what the last act will be. This can be a wonderful thing to have at an event for a few reasons.

The first reason to have a schedule is for your own benefit. Some events will be very long and the audience will begin to lose their concentration after a few hours. You'll want to give them regular breaks where they can stretch their legs and use the bathroom. Since every event has a certain flow to it, these breaks should be planned at just the right point. These intermissions should come at a time when one concept has been completely delivered but before a new one is introduced, just like acts in a play.

Some events will include a meal, and this needs to be planned for as well. You do not want to have the wait staff serving food in the middle of the keynote speaker's presentation. The meal itself will be a bit of a distraction so you may want to give the audience time to eat before moving on to the next part of the event. Don't forget to include time for clearing the tables, as this will also be a distraction.

A schedule can be just as useful for the audience. When they first come in, they'll be able to look over the schedule and see how the whole event is structured. They'll know what to expect and can plan accordingly. Someone may, for example, be particularly interested in one topic and will want to take notes. Knowing when that topic will be presented allows them enough time to be ready. Progressing through the schedule will also give the audience some sense of moving forward. It will help them feel as if the event is going quickly and smoothly.

What You Need From The Speaker

In the previous chapters, I've touched on some of the things you should get from your speaker before booking them. Many of these items are the exact same things you'll need before the event starts. Items such as products, promotional material, and a short bio or introduction are all important.

Once you've booked the speaker, however, you still need to meet with them in person before the event. It can be a good idea to do this a few days before the event, but if the speaker lives out of state you may not have that luxury. This meeting is incredibly important because you and your speaker need to be on the same page. There has to be a mutual understanding about what is expected on both ends.

Before the meeting, you should make a list of everything you'll expect from the speaker. This includes things like the length of the presentation, the endorsement of the group, and the topic of the speech. If there is anything you want the speaker to do or say, you need to let them know. Make sure they clearly understand what is expected of them so there are no arguments in the future.

You'll also want to understand what the speaker is expecting from you. Many speakers may have a set list of requirements for every event at which they speak. Your speaker might be expecting a large audience and will not be pleasantly surprised to find they are speaking at a small monthly meeting.

The following are some of the things you should discuss when you meet with your speaker:

Equipment Expectations

There will be a variety of different equipment needed for every event. Some speakers will bring their own while some will expect you to supply it. Always make sure to discuss what sort of equipment they will bring and what you'll need to have on hand. Neglecting to cover this topic can lead to a speaker showing up and being unable to deliver their presentation. This is the fastest route to failure for a REIA speaking event.

Sales/Marketing Material

First and foremost, the speaker needs to bring his or her own products. You simply can't supply this for them. You need to be clear in explaining that you expect them to bring some products and that sales will be a significant portion of the event. It can also be important to let them know if their products won't be the only ones on sale. They need to understand what type of products your group will be offering before they show up for the event.

If your speaker has their own specific order forms, then you will need these as well. Some speakers will be offering access to online material so they need to provide you with information about how this is done. In addition to this, it's important to understand any type of package deals they might be offering.

If you'd like to see an example of time tested, proven marketing materials, please shoot us an email at shaun@lifeonaire.com or larry@larrygoins.com.

Contract

Once you've discussed everything, you need to protect yourself. An oral agreement is no longer enough to ensure a successful event. While talking with your speaker, write down everything. The reason you need to do this is because you're going to put all of this information into the contract. This contract will list everything required from both sides, as clearly as possible.

What Your Speaker Needs From You

Meeting with your speaker before the event is also a great way to make sure their presentation is perfect for your group. Most speakers will be experienced in speaking to a variety of different audiences. They will likely give somewhat the same speech every time but will tailor it just a bit to be more engaging for the audience.

The following are some examples of information which can be useful for your speaker:

Experience Level of the Group

Some REIA groups consist of people new to the world of real estate investment, while others will be made up of experienced veterans. Even though the audience for the event may include non-members of your group, the event itself will probably be targeted to a specific experience level. Knowing what this level is will allow your speaker to give a presentation that speaks directly to the audience.

Estimated Size of the Audience

It's important to let your speaker know how many people you think will be at the event. Small events are vastly different from large events, particularly from the perspective of a speaker. Your speaker will want to be prepared for their presentation, and the size of the audience is one of the most important considerations. If they were planning for a small audience but show up to a room full of hundreds of people, the presentation will not go as well.

The Topic of the Meeting or Event

You'll want your speaker's presentation to be a good match for the event or meeting. There is nothing worse than having a speaker get on stage and start talking about something contradictory to the main topic of the event. If, for example, the topic is something like "Get Into Real Estate Now," you don't want a speaker who will talk about how people should get out of the real estate market.

What Other Speakers will Say

Many events will have more than one speaker. Most presentations will only last a few hours at most, so there is a need to include multiple speakers. The absolute worst thing you can do is have one speaker contradict another. The event needs to be cohesive. Each speaker should build upon and support what other speakers have said.

Anything that conflicts with what the speaker is teaching/selling will kill sales and ruin the reputation of the REIA. Imagine if one of the most reputable guys in a REIA club gets up at last month's meeting and says, "Short sales suck and I'll never do them!" Then tonight you introduce Shaun, the short sale speaker. Your speaker needs to know this so that he can combat it in his presentation.

Information about Your Group's Products

Since your group's products will be on the sales table, right next to the speaker's products, it can be a good idea to make sure your speaker is familiar with them. This is even more important when it comes to a keynote speaker. This person will be one of the major draws for the event. They may be well known and will carry a lot of credibility. Getting them to endorse your group's products can be a wonderful way to boost sales.

Simply endorsing your products isn't enough. They need to understand a bit about them so they can give an informed and honest endorsement.

Help The Speaker To Be Successful

- **Don't put unnecessary pressure on the speaker to perform—it doesn't help him/her sell more.**

I once spoke at an event where the event promoter was really putting the pressure on to sell well. This was a "for profit" REIA, and I could tell the owner was having a hard time financially. He went on and on about how well the last two speakers did, and he did so right before I went on stage. Needless to say, that adds a lot of unnecessary pressure that never equates to added sales. Granted, we sold well that night, but without the experience that I had at the time, the results could have been drastically different. Most speakers don't perform well under that kind of pressure. We know the promoter wants to us to sell well. We also want to sell well. It doesn't do any good to keep pounding it into the speaker over and over again.

- **Designate one person to help the speaker get set up.**

The best run REIAs in the country usually has one person to help the speaker get set up. This person will help with audio/visual needs, help get laptops up and running, and even provide the speaker with water, gum, and/or anything else he may need in order to have a great event. This isn't a diva thing; it's simply a matter of doing whatever is possible to have a great event. Some speakers will need a little more handholding than others. Regardless, do your best to make the speaker feel comfortable and provide him with the environment to get him comfortable and feeling good. This way, he can focus on delivering the absolute best presentation he's capable of. Trust me when I say you'll also reap the benefits as well.

- **Get the speaker started ON TIME! No later than 7:30 pm. People will leave by 9:00 pm whether he's done or not.**

Most experienced speakers know exactly how long their presentation will take from start to finish. Because of this, it's vitally important to get the speaker started on time. As a general rule of thumb, most speakers time their REIA meeting presentation to be right at 90 minutes, since this is the format most REIAs use. If you start the speaker at 7:45 instead of 7:30 because announcements went over the allotted time frame, your speaker won't finish his close until 9:15. The challenge with this is that many people will leave at 9:00 pm whether the speaker is wrapped up or not.

Again, a good speaker will overcome this by adapting his presentation to meet the new timeframe, but all of these things affect sales. If a speaker has to leave out one crucial story that's essential for his close at the end, sales will likely be affected. Start the speaker on time. Simple as that.

Review Checklist For Chapter 4

Location

☐ Is the location big enough to accommodate the estimated attendees?

☐ Is there adequate parking?

☐ Are there adequate facilities?

☐ Can it accommodate your technological needs?

☐ Can it handle any catering needs?

Technology: Do you have...

☐ A dedicated A/V person trained in the use of the equipment?

☐ An adequate PA system?

☐ Microphones to meet the needs of your speakers?

☐ A microphone for the audience?

☐ Extra batteries for the microphones?

☐ Extra microphones for back up?

☐ Projectors for either photos or videos?

☐ A simple way to operate the projectors?

☐ A large enough screen for the projectors?

☐ Wires to hook everything up?

☐ Have you tested all of the A/V equipment?

The Sales Table

☐ Do you have a dedicated sales staff?

☐ Are they experienced sales people?

☐ Do they know how to operate the payment processing systems?

☐ Are they familiar with the products and any special offers?

Do you have:

☐ Enough tables to hold all of the products?

☐ A list of all the products you'll be offering?

☐ Order forms?

☐ Pens?

☐ Clipboards?

☐ Stands for displaying products?

☐ A plan for how to organize the products?

☐ Enough products to fill demand?

☐ Promotional items?

☐ A way to collect contact information?

☐ Do you have a way to process credit and debit card payments?

☐ Have you tested this equipment?

☐ Do you have a way to handle cash sales?

☐ Can you handle online sales?

Scheduling

☐ Have you created a schedule for the event?

☐ Are there enough rest periods?

☐ Is the event organized in a cohesive way?

☐ Have you planned for the meal?

☐ Have you planned for distributing the food and collecting the plates?

What you need from the speaker

☐ Have you discussed the equipment expectations?

☐ Do you know exactly what equipment the speaker will need?

☐ Have you discussed the products the speaker will bring?

☐ Do you have all of the order forms or alternative payment methods they will use?

☐ Have you discussed the promotional material?

☐ Are you clear on the payment expectations?

☐ Is all of this outlined in the contract?

What your speaker needs from you

Do they:

☐ Understand the experience level of the group?

☐ Know the main topic of the event?

☐ Understand the local market?

☐ Know the estimated size of the audience?

☐ Know what the other speakers will talk about?

☐ Understand the type of products you'll be offering?

Chapter 5:

At The Event — How To Knock 'em Dead And Annihilate Expectations

Every successful REIA speaking event requires a fair amount of work. While the initial planning stages are important, your work is far from over once the event starts. A good event has a certain effortless flow to it. Every element leads into the next and builds to a peak of excitement, which results in a buying frenzy. This doesn't happen on its own; it requires a careful orchestration by the people running the event—ALL the people running the event. Make sure all staff and volunteers are on the same page and have the same goal in mind.

The event itself will determine if all of the time spent in the planning stages will pay off. No matter how carefully you may have considered every single detail, what happens when the audience is in the room will make or break the event. One seemingly insignificant mistake can quickly ruin the flow, which will result in a disappointed audience that simply wants to leave. This chapter will help you understand how to successfully pull off the event and what you'll need to do during it.

An Overview of Success

I've attended a lot of REIA events, both as an audience member and as a speaker. Some of them have been absolutely amazing while others were a complete disaster. What I've realized is these successful events all seem to share a few common similarities. This isn't to say every successful event was exactly the same, simply that the leaders knew what they were doing.

A good event will follow a certain formula. Timing is one of the most important elements of this formula because everything is building to a specific point. Just as with a movie, if the event takes too long to reach the dramatic climax, your audience will lose interest.

This is the basic formula for a successful event:

The Introduction Phase

The introduction phase is important because it sets the stage for the event. Some of the attendees may be unfamiliar with the group, the topic, or even the whole concept of investing. Before you can bring out a speaker who will give a detailed presentation, you have to lay the groundwork.

Early Information

Some speakers will give a presentation which covers a very specific sort of niche. To understand investing in notes, for example, the audience will need to know a bit about how notes play into the current real estate market. It's important to keep the information simple and not cover anything your speaker will be covering.

This is also the period during which other speakers will give their presentation. Every REIA speaking event should have a keynote speaker. This is the person the audience is there to see. Some larger multi-day events will have a number of different speakers and they should all go on before the main act.

Introducing the Speaker

One mistake I've seen REIA groups make is failing to properly introduce the speaker. This is an important element because it will build excitement and create a certain framework for the speaker's presentation. More on this in a minute.

The Speaker

The speaker should always be the last featured portion of the event. This person is why the audience attends the event. Your speaker is, in fact, the main reason the event exists at all. Most presentations will last roughly ninety minutes. They will spend the majority of the time delivering positive, informative content and will often end with a sales pitch and the opportunity to take what's been taught to another level.

The Sales

Once the speaker is finished, assuming the speaker has done his job well, people will begin flocking to the sales table. Hopefully, you'll experience a huge rush to the back of the room. Handling this portion of an event will take a bit of finesse, and we'll cover this in detail in the next few pages.

Looking at this layout of the event or meeting, you should be able to quickly see how everything flows together. The event starts slowly then builds momentum until the speaker comes on stage. The entire event is leading up to this last portion. When done correctly, you've empowered your speaker with the resources needed to deliver an engaging and informative presentation. A good speaker will be able to use this momentum to drive people to the sales table, inevitably increasing revenues for the REIA, providing excellent high value content, and fulfilling all purposes of the event. Now, let's break this down into each step so you know exactly what to do, and more importantly, what not to do.

Setting The Right Mood

One thing that's often overlooked by so many REIAs I've seen all around the country is setting the proper environment. The more fun people are having, the more they'll want to come back. When someone shows up to an event and you can hear a pin drop in the room, the energy level is one step away from dead. Not only is this just no fun, it doesn't do anything to help create the energy needed when the speaker gets on stage.

Regardless of the type of event, I can't stress to you the importance of building up energy in the room. Have you ever been to a restaurant that had a handful of people inside but was dead quiet? I know I have. What were your thoughts as you entered this restaurant? Did you walk in feeling like you were about to have the time of your life? Most likely you spoke to whoever you were with in a low quiet tone, hoping not to disturb the sheer silence taking place throughout the rest of the room.

Why do bars and restaurants play music? They want to create an environment that is conducive to people having a great time. Why? Because when people are having fun, they spend more money. A great time starts with environment, and environment and energy is created, in part, with sound.

What am I getting at here? Play some music at your events! I can't tell you how many events I've gone to where there were a hundred or more people in a room and the room was dead silent. At our REIA meetings and bootcamps, we crank up music over the P.A. system. We have upbeat, up-tempo music playing until it's time to start. People are socializing and networking, they're having a great time, and the energy is high. Our staff is high-fiving people as they walk in; we're having a great time, we love what we do, and it shows! This is not a funeral session; we're hosting these events to teach people how to totally transform the quality of their lives by creating wealth faster than they can create it in any other capacity! Why wouldn't we be excited about this?

Having music playing creates an environment that is fun. Even if there are only ten people in the room, a room with music being played just seems like more fun than a room without it. It all starts with perception, and sound in the room creates the perception of activity and fun.

We have a large playlist of music consisting of upbeat music that just about everyone loves. We hook up the iPod, make sure the song list is on repeat, and let it play. And we turn it up! Don't get me wrong; we don't play it so loud in the room that you can't carry on a conversation. We want people talking to each other. But we do turn it up and get the energy moving in the room. And the best part is, people love it! We get people all the time that tell us how much they enjoy our events just because they get to learn and have a great time in the process. That starts with the environment that you create. People are talking, they're laughing, and they're having a good time. And when new people come for the first time, they come back. Not only was the information great during the meeting, but also because we create an environment that makes it much easier to meet other people before the meeting even started.

Every once in a while we'll get that one person with something negative to say about the fact that there's upbeat music and that everyone is having just too much fun. Well, I guess you can't please everyone. But I'll tell you this—the other 99.9% of people love it!

Before The Speaker Goes On Stage

What you need to do before the speaker gets on stage will often be determined by the type of event. If this is more than a typical monthly meeting then you may handle it a little differently than you would handle a regular REIA meeting. The process is fairly simple: welcome everyone to the meeting, cover any important announcements, and then lead right into introducing the featured speaker. The audience is there for the speaker, so get right into it. I went to a movie recently with my wife, and I timed how long it took for the actual movie to start. We got there at 7 pm, since that's the time the movie was supposed to start. By the time we got through all of the commercials and previews for other movies coming soon, it was 7:26 before we got to the opening credits of the actual movie we came to see. I'm all for previews, but 26 minutes? Really?

When you're doing an event with a selling speaker, it's important that you get them started as quickly as possible. Many REIA meetings run with a schedule similar to what you see below for a weeknight meeting. Of course, larger weekend events with multiple speakers will look drastically different from what you see below, but once you understand what happens during a general meeting, planning a larger event will be that much easier. (We'll break each one of these timeframes down further in a moment.)

- **6:00 pm to 7:00 pm**: Open Networking

- **7:00 pm to 7:30 pm**: Official meeting begins. Announcements take place, forced networking and "Haves and Wants" take place (more on this in a minute). Host gets audience pumped up, ready for the main speaker. Host announces main speaker.

- **7:30 pm to 9:00 pm**: Featured Speaker takes the stage, provides great training, then towards the end of the presentation, drives people to the back of room to sign up for whatever package(s) are offered.

- **9:00 pm to 9:20 pm**: People flock to the back table, fill out order forms, payments are processed, and purchasers are delivered products and given instructions on what to do next (if anything).

- **9:30 pm**: Event is over. Begin clearing out the room/cleanup, etc...

6-7 pm - Open Networking

People love to network with other investors. Leave time for it before the official meeting starts. I've seen a lot of REIA clubs provide food during this time, which is a great hook for getting people into the room early. Not only does this provide for great networking time, it also helps to get your main meeting started on time. If done correctly, the members will have to get to the REIA meeting early or else there won't be any food left.

At our REIA meeting, we make sure to order enough food so there's none left around 6:45 or so. People love the food and love the networking, so they try to get there early so they don't miss out on either one. Sure the food costs a little bit of money each month, but it's worth the price. Plus, you don't even have to pay for it if you're smart. Get a sponsor like a title company or lender to pay for the food, then give them credit for doing so at the beginning of the meeting. It might sound something like this: "Hey everyone, thanks for coming! Did you guys like the food and drinks we had this evening? Well, let's give a big thank you round of applause to our friends at ABC Title Company for paying for the food for all of us to enjoy! Thank you ABC Title Company!" (round of applause starts) "By the way, we close our deals at ABC Title company because they have never let us down, they do a great job for us, and they've helped us make a LOT of money this year! So thanks for the food, and thanks for doing a great job, guys."

Simple as that. You just got people to come early and it cost you nothing. You also just gave a great plug to ABC Title Company which will make them come back to buy the food every single month. Does that mean this is all ABC Title Company pays for to be considered the featured title company for the REIA? Not necessarily. Some REIAs will have them pay for the food and pay an additional fee for being the "recommended" title company. That's up to you. But it's a great way to get free food, which gets people there early, and gets the meeting started on time.

7 pm - Official Meeting Begins

- **The Host/Kicking off the meeting the RIGHT way**

No matter what type of event you may be hosting, building excitement is crucial. Whoever is opening the event needs to have a pulse.

Okay, they probably need a little more than just a pulse, but I've seen some MC's of events that I wasn't sure even had that to work with. The host absolutely must be enthusiastic! The energy has to be there. This positive attitude is incredibly contagious and the audience will begin to emulate the enthusiasm. When people first arrive, they'll be eager to hear the promised information so you'll want to keep that desire strong right from the start.

Here's what I mean. I once attended a taping of the David Letterman show in New York City. The show, as you probably know, is filmed in front of a live studio audience as many shows like this are. The producers need the audience to be lively, upbeat, and laughing at Dave's jokes. What you don't get to see when you watch shows like this on TV is the warm-up act. None of these shows starts immediately; they always begin with a whole session designed to warm up the audience first. Someone will come on stage and start building excitement for the show by telling jokes to get the audience in the mood for comedy. They might interact with the audience to get them engaged, ask questions that solicit funny responses, etc... The band will usually come on stage even before that and play some upbeat music (which, by the way, is usually very loud). All of these things play into how well the audience will respond when Dave Letterman actually comes out and takes the stage.

A successful show requires an audience with a ton of energy. A host doesn't just stand up and speak to a cold audience, he will always do a better job coming into a room with an audience that is already excited to see him, ready and eager for what's about to take place. Dave feeds off of the energy of the audience. It makes him a better comedian. It makes the show more fun. If the audience is dead, the show will also be dead. Granted, Dave needs to bring his own energy into the room as well, but it all starts with setting the environment up front. That starts with the opening act. If you're a REIA owner, chances are, you're the opening act.

Some of you will try to be the headliner (Dave) when you shouldn't be. Remember, people came to the David Letterman show to see David Letterman; they didn't come to see the opening act guy. The opening act guy is vitally important to the show as a whole, but he serves his purpose of setting the mood and then moves out of the way so Dave can do his thing. Dave's purpose is to make people laugh and keep them entertained. The speakers "thing" at your REIA meeting is to do a lot of what Dave does, but also to sell stuff. It's hard to sell stuff to a cold audience. It's even harder to sell stuff if the opening act keeps interjecting and taking the focus from the headliner. There's a reason David Letterman runs the show the way he runs it. His way works.

Not everyone can be the opening act/front of the room pump-up person. Some of you shouldn't be the opening act. It just doesn't fit your personality. If this is the case, you may not be the right person for the job. Don't get me wrong, it doesn't mean that you are incapable of running a well-oiled machine of a REIA group. You may be the best organizer of people, of income, of bookkeeping, of many things that are also necessary to build a well-run REIA. However, just because you're good at many of those things doesn't necessarily make you the best person for the front of the room.

I spoke for a rather large event once where the organizer of the event was among the best I've ever seen—at organizing the event, that is! This guy knew how to market to draw a crowd. He knew how to book the greatest speakers in the country. He knew how every room should be set up, how to lead the entire organization and more, and he did these things very well. But when he got up to the front of the room to announce every speaker that entire weekend, the energy in the room totally and completely died. This guy might as well have had one foot in the grave. He was excellent at everything else that was required to put on an incredible event, but he was the worst MC that I've ever seen. It killed the energy in the room.

Every speaker that weekend had to bring their "A game" even more than usual. We each had to work twice as hard to win the hearts of the audience because when we each got up to speak, the room was totally dead. They were dead because they were taught to be this way by the promoter. Just because someone can or will do a job doesn't mean they should do that job. Make sense?

What's true for the David Letterman show is true for REIA events as well. It doesn't matter how exciting or experienced a speaker is, their job is going to be ten times harder if they walk out to a cold, unresponsive audience.

My friend, Steve Cook, shared a story with me recently how he sold very well at the Wisconsin REIA located in Milwaukee. One of the reasons he sold so well is because of the introduction given by promoter and REIA owner, Eric Lundbergh. Not only did Eric bring a boatload of energy into the room, he also shared a personal story of how Steve affected his life personally. He went on to say that he wouldn't be where he is today had it not been for Steve. This set the mood for the entire evening and basically said to the audience, "If you want your life to change too, you'd better listen to everything Steve has to say." (And buy his stuff.)

Wendy Patton, another national speaker who also owns a "for profit" REIA in Michigan, recently introduced me to her REIA when I spoke there. It was among one of the best intro's I've ever heard. Not only does Wendy give 100% of her heart and soul in the way she presents herself, she also shared personal stories explaining all that my teachings had done for her personally. She gave example after example of how my presentation changed her perspective and got her to a whole new level. She pre-framed the audience, telling them that they are getting ready to hear something that will totally and completely change their life, but only if they implement it and take action on it this evening. By the time I got on stage, the entire audience was on the edge of their seats, dying to hear what I was going to share with them.

Alan Langston, the owner of AZREIA located in Phoenix, Arizona also gave a phenomenal intro. When I went there to speak on short sales, not only did he give a great introduction saying that I was the most sought after short sale expert in the entire country, he also planned ahead. The meeting the month before I spoke was all about market changes, where the marketing had been, and where it was headed. Literally one month prior to me coming in to speak, Alan was prepping the audience by discussing the importance of short sales, how they are an inevitable part of investing, and how every investor needs to know how to make money doing them. Absolutely brilliant. It's no wonder why we did close to six figures in sales while I was there.

While we are talking about Alan and AZREIA, Alan has a very large group and knows how to market, so when I go speak for Alan, he asks me to host a three-day bootcamp for him as follow up training for his members. Alan also participates in the revenue from the boot-camp sales, and we hold the event at his corporate office in Phoenix, Arizona. This is a great way to offer additional training for your members as long as your group is large enough to make it feasible.

Last but not least before moving forward, keep the room temperature a bit on the cold side. The truth is, you'll sell far more to a room that's slightly cool than you ever will to a room that's warm or hot. When people get hot, they get cranky. When they're slightly cold, they perk up, pay attention, and buy more stuff. We've tested this over and over again. Keep the room slightly cool. If it sounds like I'm being picky with this one, this is not a matter of being a diva—warm rooms affect sales. If you think it's going to be an issue with your audience, warn them in advance of the event that the room is a bit chilly and to bring layers of clothing. I once sat in on a Tony Robbins event where I personally witnessed him close about 40% of a room of more than 3,000 people on a $10,000 product. The room was so cold you could just about see your breath.

Was that the only factor that helped with sales? Of course not, but it was one important factor, and it was very well thought out and planned in advance.

Give the Information

Okay, so the energy in the room is high, your energy is high, and you're ready to start the meeting! First things first, you'll want to give the audience a quick intro as to who you are (notice I said quick), what the REIA group is all about, the topic of the event, and what they have to look forward to over the course of the evening or day. This is called pre-framing, and it is important to build the excitement within the room.

A lot of people say to under promise and over deliver, which I agree with in many cases; however, when giving an intro for what's to come at a REIA meeting event with a speaker, I'd rather you over promise and over deliver! People will only get as excited as you give them a reason to be excited. The best meetings are the ones where the host says (with absolute confidence) that the audience is in for a huge treat, that what they're going to learn at this meeting will be life-changing if they'll implement it, that it will be worth their time for being here. This sets the expectations high and the anticipation higher. This is a good thing!

Now you can begin to get into the meeting itself. To put it simply, if the audience doesn't know who you are or why they should listen to you, they won't place any value on your endorsement of the speaker. But you must do this quickly. There's still a lot more to do and the clock is ticking.

Forced Networking

Some REIA clubs do what I call "forced networking," and I think it's a great idea if done correctly and quickly.

The way it works is simple. Let's say there are 100 people in the room. You can either count off each person in the room into groups, starting from 1 and ending at 10, then starting over, OR, you can hand out raffle tickets if you're giving away attendance prizes at the meeting and use the last number on the ticket to assign numbers to people. Basically, each person in the room now has a number from 1 through 10 assigned to them. Before the meeting you will have set up ten little signs spread out to locations numbered 1 – 10 throughout the room, and whatever number each person has been assigned is where they go when directed. This means you'll have ten little mini-groups consisting of ten people in each group spread out around the room. Once the host blows his whistle, each person within each group gets one minute to share with the other nine people in their group who they are, why they're at the meeting, and what they can offer that will benefit the others in the group.

This is a great strategy because it gets everyone talking about their favorite subject—themselves. It also forces people to get to know others in the room. This has several benefits. First, it gets the newbies in the room meeting experienced people they might not have otherwise met. This increases repeat attendance and helps people want to come back. Second, it gives people a chance to talk about how they can help others at the REIA and promotes a community environment. At our meetings, we have all kinds of people get up and let the others know how they can help one another. One person may get up and say, "I'm John Smith. I'm a rehabber, and I can help each of you by letting you know who some of the best contractors and staging companies are. Here's my card." Another person may say something like, "Hi, I'm Janet and I'm a real estate attorney, so if any of you need help evicting tenants that aren't paying, I can help you with that."

When we surveyed our members, we found that this one feature is what kept both newbies and experienced investors coming back each month. The reason for this is because it focused on getting everyone in the room what they want. Some people are there for the education. Some are there for the networking. Some are there to loan money to others. Some are there to wholesale deals. Why not encourage all of these things? Believe it or not, this "forced networking" actually increases sales as well, since it starts the meeting off on the right foot.

"Have's and Wants" Networking

"Haves and Wants" is another form of networking that's very valuable to your audience. I've seen many REIAs do a version of this, but it basically works like this:

The host of the meeting explains that "Haves and Wants" is a quick session where anyone in the room can have a microphone for 30 seconds and share anything they have that could benefit others in the room (could be a property for sale, a service they offer, etc...) or want (they're looking for rental properties that are 2-3 bedrooms in Jefferson County, etc...).

It's simple, but it gets the energy up in the room and if done correctly, it can be done in ten minutes. It's a great way to start out a meeting if people in the room are active investors and doing deals. If your room is not as active and consists more of new investors, you might be better of sticking with "forced networking" discussed above.

Keep in mind that if you want to get your main speaker started on time, it's going to be really hard to squeeze in "forced networking" and also have time for "Haves and Wants." You may choose to pick one or the other, so that you can wrap up quickly and get to the main event.

Questions

Questions are a common part of many presentations. Some people will develop questions based solely on the information being presented. These people will be eager to have their questions answered and may even fixate on them throughout the entire presentation. It's important to keep these people from interrupting the speaker. Let the audience know that they should save all questions for a later time.

A good speaker will know how to defer questions in a way that's professional and non-confrontational. As a speaker, I welcome a lot of questions during an all-day Saturday workshop, because we have a full eight hours together. During a weeknight 90-minute presentation, however, a few questions from the audience could take the presentation in an entirely different direction, not leaving enough time for what the audience came for. More importantly, it may not leave enough time for the close and could destroy sales.

Some speakers will include a question and answer portion in their presentation. This needs to be handled in an organized manner. Setting up a specific microphone for the audience can be an excellent solution. Audience members can line up behind the microphone and have their questions answered one by one. Either that, or sometimes speakers will ask for a "mic runner" to bring to people so they can ask questions from their seats. This format works well in a packed house with not much room to walk in between aisles. Try to avoid having the audience yell out questions from their seats, because this will quickly dissolve into chaos. Instead, if you're going to have a mic runner, make sure the audience knows to raise their hand, and if they're called on a mic runner will come to them.

Giveaways and attendance prizes?

If you're going to do any attendance or door prizes you MUST do this before the main speaker takes the stage. DO NOT FOR ANY REASON save things like this for the end of the meeting. This will kill your sales. We'll talk about this more in a moment.

Also, when it comes to giving away prizes, the whole "bring the energy to the room" thing applies here as well. Remember, you're giving away awesome free stuff! You should be excited about this! If you're not, get someone else who is excited to give away the stuff. I've been to meetings where they do the raffle, announce a winner, and no one claps, no one is excited, and no one even says thank you. This is prime time to build up the energy in the room by commanding a response. If you're thinking, "Command a response? It sounds harsh to me," I understand. I'm not talking about being a drill sergeant. I mean you should encourage clapping for the winner by starting to clap a little bit yourself. Others will follow your lead. If you don't initiate the clap, no one else will. If you clap, everyone will. Try it; you'll see what I mean.

And if I clap and only a few others join in, I might even command more of a response—just by having some fun with it. I might say something like, "Come on guys! Jason just won a $50 gift certificate to Home Depot! Show him by round of applause how much it should have been you that won!"

Drive them to the Saturday Workshop

Right before the speaker goes on stage might also be a great time to mention any follow-up events like Saturday workshops. Be sure to only mention information that's going to build up the attendance of this particular speaker's event. Do not mention anything else for sale, other than what the featured speaker will be promoting. I personally witnessed a REIA host spend the entire half hour before I went on stage promoting a bus tour that he was going to be doing the following month. He said over and over again how the bus tour was going to teach them everything they needed to know about how to evaluate real estate deals, and that they didn't need any other training to be successful in their business. The bus tour was $99 and he was pushing it hard. This was right before I was getting ready to offer a $1997 home study course and bootcamp package.

I'm all for promoting a REIA's other things, like local bus tours, other local coaching programs, etc.... Just don't do it during a meeting where you're having a selling speaker also offering something for sale. Anything else that is offered is simply a distraction to the products presented by the selling speaker that night. Do not offer any other products before or after a speaker is getting ready to sell. It won't help either sale. Remember, a confused mind says "no," and offering up multiple choices of things people can buy will only negatively affect both offers.

If I'm hosting one of my Wednesday night REIA meetings and our featured speaker is staying over to do a Saturday workshop also, I'll likely mention the Saturday workshop before I make the official introduction and pass the torch.

If I'm the speaker at an event, I usually bring up the Saturday workshop again numerous times in my presentation also. The key is to get everyone in the room to also come to the Saturday workshop. The reason for this is that, as a speaker, I may only have 90 minutes to speak and sell my product during the Wednesday night REIA meeting, but if I'm also doing a Saturday workshop, I may have a full eight hours in the front of the room. That extra time helps me build a lot more credibility within the audience, I can share more information, and honestly, I can sell higher priced products like bootcamps and close a higher percentage of the room. Because of this, I'll mention it many times throughout my 90-minute presentation.

If I had a choice between speaking at a Wednesday night REIA meeting or doing an all-day Saturday workshop REIA meeting, I'd choose the Saturday workshop every time. It's not because I just love working on Saturdays! It's because the sales are almost always significantly better.

Two side notes you should make about Saturday workshops. First, as a REIA owner, your job is to do everything you can do to make sure the workshop is a success and that people stay in the room for the entire duration of the event. This means you should consider providing lunch to everyone that attends. This will ensure that the audience stays there and gets everything the event is designed to provide for them.

When I first started speaking, I did a Saturday workshop where we broke for lunch at noon and told everyone to be back in the room by 1:00. Sure enough 1:00 came and only about 20% of the people were back in their seats. Come to find out, every restaurant in the area was packed. Getting food took forever. Then for everyone to pay their checks took even longer. We were finally able to get started again when everyone got back to the room, but the clock had ticked all the way up to 1:45 before everyone was ready to go again. Not only that, but some people were so frustrated with lunch taking so long, they figured they missed too much of the meeting so they didn't even come back.

Nowadays, we include lunch into the cost of the Saturday workshop. This is such key factor in the day that I've been known to buy lunch for an entire room of audience members just to get them to stay there. If I have 100 people in the room and lunch costs me $1,000, that can be recouped with just one sale of a home study course. But if I lose five people because lunch took too long... you get the idea.

Secondly, if your REIA meets on the first Monday of every month and you want a nationally recognized speaker to come do a Saturday workshop as well, that's a pretty long stretch for a speaker to stay in town to serve your REIA. Most speakers don't want to stay in town by themselves that long, and may decide to make two trips. Some speakers don't want to make two trips since this comes with two complete travel schedules, two sets of airline tickets, hotels, etc., so some of them will tell you they will do one meeting or the other. Another option is to have the Saturday event 2-3 weeks after the monthly meeting. This gives you time to promote it more to fill the room.

If you want speakers to do both a weeknight REIA meeting and a Saturday workshop, you'll draw better speakers if your weeknight meeting is on a Wednesday or Thursday night. That way, you can immediately follow up the weeknight REIA meeting with a Saturday workshop and not make the speaker's travel schedule any more hectic than it may already be.

Don't get me wrong, I'm not saying you have to change the date your REIA meets. I'm not even suggesting that every speaker is going to have a problem with it if your meetings are, in fact, on Monday nights. I'm just saying you may have a harder time getting some of the bigger fish to do both, so it's something to consider.

Leave Time for the Speaker

Okay, now that we've gotten all the usual stuff out of the way, it's time to introduce your speaker. Before we do, I can't stress to you how important it is to get the speaker on stage on time. Many speakers have their presentation timed to the minute. They know exactly how long it takes to go from the start of the presentation to the final close. When you run over and make the speaker start late, you're inadvertently killing sales. When 9 pm comes, some people will leave the room whether the speaker is done with his close or not. The last thing you want to do is make the speaker run late because you started him late.

I get it that being the front of the room person is a lot of fun to those of us who enjoy getting in front of an audience. We all like sharing our own experiences and helping others become successful. The problem is, some hosts love it just a little too much. Some of you (you may know who you are, you may not) love to hear yourselves talk just a little too much.

There was a REIA owner that had a phenomenal association for a long time, but the owner would get up at the front of the room before a national speaker went on stage and talk about her dog for a half hour. With all respect, no one came to the event to hear about your dog! They came to see the headlined speaker! Get him on stage, and do it in a timely manner.

Last but not least, if you don't know how long the speaker plans on presenting, ask. If you've done what we've taught you to do in this book and have a contractual agreement with your speaker, you should already know how long he plans to speak, but it wouldn't be a bad idea to confirm with him one last time before the meeting starts, just to make sure you're getting him started on time. Generally speaking, most speakers are allotted a minimum ninety minutes. Have fun with this, but keep one eye on the clock and always leave enough room for your speaker.

Introducing the Speaker

Introducing the speaker is an important time in any REIA event. There is a delicate art to the way a speaker is successfully introduced. Doing it correctly will set the stage for your speaker, leaving them with an energetic audience, eager to absorb the speaker's information. Incorrectly introducing the speaker, on the other hand, can have a serious impact on their credibility as well as their ability to help promote sales.

Everything trickles down. This is a rule. Remember, if you're engaging, active, and eager to bring the speaker on stage, your audience will feel the same way. If you're disinterested and come across as bored out of your mind, the audience will also react the same way. Your speaker is relying on you to create a good audience. This makes the introduction one of the most important elements in any event.

• Who Should Do It?

The person you select to handle the introduction is every bit as important as what they say. A good analogy for this can be found in celebrity endorsements. Marketing agencies will hire a well-known celebrity to endorse a product because it allows them to piggyback on that person's credibility. A sports star, for example, is the perfect person to promote athletic equipment because they are known as a world-class athlete.

The person who handles the introduction should—hopefully—be well known by the group. If at all possible, this should not be someone who requires their own introduction. They should also be well respected and admired by the members of your group. This is someone the group looks up to. Members trust this person; they believe the things he says. When he is excited for something, they will get excited for the same thing.

More importantly, having this person introduce the speaker is one way to endorse not only the speaker but their information and products as well. When you have a familiar, respected leader of the group introduce a speaker, the audience will instantly transfer this person's credibility onto the speaker. There will be no need for the speaker to establish themselves because you've already given them the seal of approval.

• Memorize The Bio

Most introductions will require a little bit of information. This can be as simple as who the speaker is, but can also be as complex as some history about their career. You'll get all of this information from the speaker's bio, which, if you've done what we've taught you to do, they should have given to you before the event. The person introducing the speaker should have this information memorized and be able to deliver it without being the boring guy reading it from a card. (Bueller? Bueller?)

I've been to REIA events where the leaders read the introduction word for word. This makes it impossible to fully endorse a speaker. The audience will feel as if the host is unfamiliar with the speaker.

When this happens, the audience naturally becomes skeptical, which will cause them to question the information, rather than absorbing it.

Reading directly from the bio is also incredibly unprofessional. One of the most important elements in hosting a successful REIA event is making everything feel as professional as possible. (Just because an environment is professional doesn't mean it's no fun. You can and should have both!) This might require some rehearsal, just like any public performance. If you get on stage and start reading from an index card, it will seem as if you weren't ready and this will reflect back on the group.

Always make sure to memorize the bio or introduction. Practice delivering it with energy and enthusiasm. Remember that everything trickles down from the top, so your ability to be excited for the speaker will determine how excited your audience is.

• Give Them A Real Endorsement

While the bio will give you some information about who the speaker is, you'll still need to give them a strong endorsement. Your speaker is relying on your ability to transfer credibility. They need you—or whoever is introducing them—to personally approve of the material and information they've brought. Without this endorsement, they will need to waste time qualifying themselves to the audience. A third party endorsement (from you) is always much better than me as a speaker trying to tell the audience how good I am. When you say it, it's a testimony. When I say it, it just comes across as bragging and being conceited.

If you're at this point in the process, then you've done a lot of work to make the event a reality. You've planned every detail and scoured the world to find the best possible speaker. Let the audience know! A strong endorsement should leave the audience feeling as if this person is rare. Your group doesn't invite just anyone to speak. Let them know how selective you are in choosing a speaker. Tell them you wouldn't bring someone on stage unless the information they have is extremely valuable.

This is why it's so important to have a respected member handle the introduction. Someone who is admired by the group will come with instant clout. The group will place value on what this person says and will not dismiss it lightly. When this person endorses your speaker, the audience will accept it without question.

• Authority

We talked about this briefly earlier—let's expand a bit. One of the most vital things that happens during the introduction is establishing the speaker as an authority on the subject matter and an authority from the front of the room. The audience is there to hear valuable information directly from an expert in the field. They want to hear real information, not something which has been filtered and regurgitated by someone else. If they would listen to any person, simply because that person read a book, there would be no need for the event at all. Your transfer of authority is important.

The speaker must be considered the authority in whatever they're speaking on. This is someone who has experienced a significant level of success in the real world (or failure and managed to turn it around), someone who has managed to develop their own strategies. Your speaker is someone who has written books, produced videos, and even created courses about this subject. They have been nationally recognized, spoken on stages with other celebrities, whatever you can use to build up their credibility and authority from the front of the room. Of course, be honest with the information you're sharing, but no matter what, make sure to help the audience understand why you're willing to hand over this authority to the speaker. When you do, you'll be empowering the speaker with the support they need to give the absolute best presentation possible. Not only will this affect the presentation, it will also positively affect sales as well.

The final transfer of authority must be physical. What I mean is this; once you've made the introduction, wait for the speaker to get to the front of the room, walk on stage, then either give him a handshake (or sometimes even a quick hug may be appropriate depending on the situation), and then exit the stage immediately. Your job is now done for the next ninety minutes. The handshake, as simple as it sounds, is important and is a physical sign to show that you've now given up the stage (and the authority of the front of the room) willingly to your speaker.

A Really Bad Speaker's Intro Example

I've seen some bad intros in my day, and I'm sure you have as well. Here are a few characteristics of a terrible intro for a speaker. (You may laugh, but this is a real example!)

- The host looks like a bum on the street, has no energy, is boring to listen to, even worse to look at, and comes across as someone that struggles with depression each and every waking moment of his life.

- The host reads directly from the speaker's bio, mumbling the words, not speaking loudly enough for the people in the back of the room to hear what he's saying. He has no idea who the speaker is in reality or why the audience should listen to him, and doesn't provide any reason for the audience to have any emotional attachment to anything they're about to hear.

- The host appears to be somewhere in the neighborhood of 150 years old, even though he is only 34.

- The host tells a story in a monotone voice for more than 25 minutes about his need for coffee in the morning, and how he does nothing without a few cups before he gets to work each day, which led to his divorce. His wife just doesn't need coffee. She's a morning person.

- The host then tells a barrage of other stories about things that don't matter to anyone else in the room but him, and makes the featured speaker start his presentation more than 15 minutes behind schedule.

I'm about three minutes away from killing myself just by remembering this guy! Okay, that's an extreme example, but you get the idea.

I was speaking in Texas one night and they had a lady board member of the group introduce me. The introduction was so bad that I turned to the guy standing beside me at the back of the room and said "Was that my introduction?" He said, "I really couldn't tell." The only way we realized that it was is she started looking for me in the room and saying, "Where is Larry?

Another quick story about reading the introduction. I was at another group a while back and the REIA group owner read my introduction word for word in a monotone. And my introduction even starts by advising the person introducing me that they need to be enthusiastic and upbeat and learn the introduction in advance so it doesn't look like it is being read. As soon as I came on stage I said, "Wow, thanks for that great introduction; you could hardly tell you were reading it." Then everyone started laughing, but he got the point.

A Great Speaker's Intro Example

A phenomenal intro would be more like one that I experienced recently when speaking for Wendy Patton, a national speaker who also owns a REIA in Michigan. She invited me to come speak to her group, and she knows better than anyone how to give a phenomenal intro. This isn't word for word because we didn't record this particular event, but it sounded something like this.

"Guys, you are in for a real treat tonight! Our featured speaker, Shaun McCloskey is someone I've known personally for more than ten years now. He was actually an attendee of a bootcamp I taught back in Phoenix, Arizona when he first got started investing, and it's been so awesome to see him grow over the years from being a brand new investor, like some of you may be tonight, to the absolute success he has become today. Not only has he personally closed more than 300 real estate flips during that time, he's also got a great family and built his entire real estate business putting them first. I've never met someone that knows how to make the money he's going to show you guys how to make tonight while also having freedom with his time as well! What I love most about him is that he not only teaches from the heart, he also teaches you the real life stuff that no one else teaches. What I mean is that anyone can show you guys how to make a lot money, but very few people can show you how to have a life in the process. I struggled with that personally until I, myself, started getting personal coaching from Shaun. Can you believe that? The student became the teacher!

"Shaun does not speak at REIAs like this often, everyone, and I can't even begin to tell you how blessed we are to have him here tonight. Are you guys ready to learn from my coach how to not only make a ridiculous income this year, but also have more free time than you've ever had before, to do the things you love the most? Then please put your hands together and let's give the warmest welcome anyone has ever gotten here at Michigan REIA, and welcome my coach and great friend, Mr. Shaun McCloskey!"

Now THAT was one heck of an introduction. I hadn't even gotten on stage yet and was already getting a standing ovation from everyone in the room! The energy was there already; the entire night was set up correctly; we gave a great presentation to a ready, willing and participatory audience, and the sales were great, too! All because Wendy knows how to set up the speaker properly.

By the way, nothing she did took away her own authority as the REIA owner. If anything, it complimented what's she's doing with the REIA. She did a great job of building me up and built the credibility right from the start. This only made her look better, too.

This may be an extreme example. Not all of you will have known the speaker for ten years. Most of you won't be getting personal coaching from the speaker. But replace those things with other things that matter to you and the audience and make it personal. It will make all the difference in the world.

Get Everything Out Of The Way

The most important thing to remember is to keep the speaker for the end. This final portion of the event should not be interrupted by anything. Once the speaker is finished with their presentation, the event is over. Nothing, other than the sales portion, should happen after the keynote speaker, hence the importance of getting everything out of the way beforehand.

If you want people to sign up to a mailing list, make sure to do it early. Doing a raffle? Do it early. Sharing info about the sponsors? Do it early (and make sure the sponsor's message doesn't conflict with the speaker's message). Celebrating Marge's 95th birthday? Do it early. If you've forgotten to do something before the speaker gets on stage, you'll be forced to drop it completely. Trust me on this one; do not under any circumstance get back on stage after you've handed the mic over to the main speaker. This sounds crazy, I know, but when you're at the front of the room you have the authority of the room. When you announce another speaker and hand him the mic, you are essentially handing over, with your permission, the authority of the room. Any time you jump in and try to interject, you're taking away that authority from the front of the room again. This affects sales. Big time.

Try to remember that you're hiring a speaker for multiple reasons. If you've chosen well, your speaker will be able to fill all of these requirements. You do, however, have to let them do their job. The excitement they create is a temporary frame of mind for the audience. By interjecting once the speaker has the mic, you're preventing people from acting on it (especially important at the end of their presentation during the close), and will be unintentionally undoing everything your speaker has achieved.

During The Presentation

At this point, all of your hard work is paying off. The seats are filled, the sales table is stocked, the audience is pumped up ready to see the main act, and the speaker is about to come on stage. This is what everything has been leading up to. What you need to do now is let it happen as smoothly as you can.

Here's typically how the presentation might look:

- **7:30 PM - Featured Speaker Begins**

Technology

Make sure all of the necessary technology is set up and ready to go before you introduce the speaker. You don't want to introduce the speaker and then be setting up while they're talking. Most importantly, the technology needs to be ready to go right away, without the need to test it or troubleshoot while the speaker is on stage.

In some cases, you may need to have your own Power Point presentation up on the screen for the announcements; you will then need to switch over to the speaker's Power Point at some point. This way, you'll be able to keep yourself on track, recognize the sponsors of the REIA, etc. But the speaker will likely have his own presentation on his own laptop, and the last thing you want to do is introduce the speaker and then force him to spend the first 3-5 minutes of his presentation changing out your laptop for his and resetting everything up. Not only does this kill all of the energy in the room, it's just unprofessional. The best thing to do is have whoever is responsible for the audio/video of the event to come up and change things out beforehand. That way, the person making the announcements doesn't have to stop what he's doing and make the changes in the middle of talking, and the speaker won't have to do it either. It sounds simple, but it makes for a much better meeting.

Remember that some speakers may need multiple types of technology. They may, for example, need to switch between playing a video and showing examples from their computer. Make sure all of this is set up before the introduction. Stopping to change everything in the middle of the speech will damage the entire event. Some speakers hinge their entire closing portion of their presentation on video testimonials, which means both the audio and video must work correctly.

Internet access is another challenge that may come up. If you're having a speaker that's selling an internet-based product, and a big part of his presentation revolves around showing people how his website works, you must test the internet connection in the room ahead of time. In addition to making sure you can actually get internet access in the room, you're going to want to check on the price of internet at the location of the event as well. A good friend of mine showed up to do a presentation at a hotel that charged him $1,000 per day for internet access. It was obviously an unplanned expense, but necessary in order for him to present his product. Another speaker friend of mine showed up to give a presentation on the importance of technology and the internet connection was so bad that he had to skip 70% of his presentation waiting on each page to load properly. Not a very good example of how awesome technology can be!

I can't stress to you the importance of testing each of these things before the meeting starts to make sure everything will work as it should. Without trying to come across as negative, you must plan for the worst-case scenario. Why, you ask? Well, when it comes to technology, Murphy's Law almost always applies: "Anything that can go wrong probably will."

Handouts

Many speakers will have some sort of printed information to be distributed to the audience. This can be examples to help support their information or worksheets which the audience is supposed to fill out. Longer events, such as multi-day seminars and bootcamps, are even more likely to include handouts of some kind and you need to plan for this.

Make sure you understand and are prepared for everything that will need to be handed out before the speaker goes on stage. The best way to handle this sort of thing is to consider distributing the materials before the event begins. One great solution is to place a copy at each seat so people can look through it when they first sit down. The last thing you want to do is create a situation where the speaker needs to stop, as everyone crowds around the person handing out the papers. This takes away the focus from the front of the room, which also negatively affects sales.

Pump Up The REIA - Encourage Memberships

Not every speaker does what I'm about to share with you, but every one of them should.

When I'm speaking at an event, one of the first things I do at the beginning of the presentation is acknowledge the organization and the host of the event. I also make sure to promote the idea of everyone in the audience becoming a member of the REIA. It may sound something like this:

"I'd like to take a quick moment to acknowledge Mike and Christina for running such a fine example of a real estate investors association! I don't know if you guys know this or not, but it takes a lot of planning and hard work to put on an event like this, and how awesome is this country where we can go to a meeting once per month and learn how to be millionaires?"

At this point, I'll start clapping, applauding the owners and/or board members of the REIA, and everyone else in the room will follow suit and do the same.

"Mike and Christina are two of the best examples I've seen of really doing their research to bring in the best of the best speakers from around the country to provide the best education on the planet! You should see the interview process they made me go through just to be here tonight! By the way, how many of you are members of the association?" (Hands go up.) "Good! How many of you are not members yet?" (Hands go up.) "Okay, great. Listen, every single one of you that put your hands up and aren't a member needs to become a member tonight. I'm not paid to tell you that, and I get nothing for encouraging you to become a member, but it's that important! And to prove to you how strongly I feel about this group being such a big contributor to your success, I have a free gift I'd like to provide to anyone here that decides to become a member tonight. Fair?"

The free gift can be anything of value, as long as it's not the main product you're getting ready to sell that night. You also don't want the free gift to sway anyone who signs up to become a member from also buying your course that day as well. Keep it simple— something with high-perceived value that can really benefit new members. Make sure everyone knows what the free gift is and is okay with it. (Most REIAs encourage and love when I offer to do this. Only one REIA has ever asked me not to offer this since they already have their own promotion for new members and didn't feel the need to add to it.) It not only boosts membership signups, but the REIA owners usually really appreciate it.

If the speaker you booked doesn't offer this up to you, ask him about it. Many speakers will be happy to provide something to encourage membership to your group.

After The Speaker

As you now know, the speaker is the last portion of the event. Experienced speakers with a product to sell during their presentation will most often end their speech with an offer, explaining how the audience members can take their education beyond what they've just learned. They will endorse the products on the sales table, and may even use a free promotional item to drive people to the back of the room.

No matter what, never stop this momentum. This means your job is, quite frankly, to shut up and not say a word! I don't mean to sound harsh, but I want to make sure you really get this! If your speaker did his job correctly, the audience will be rushing over to the sales table. I've seen event leaders stop the audience, tell them to sit back down, and then proceed to cover something truly inconsequential and unnecessary. The only thing this achieves is a massive reduction in sales.

Resist the urge to wrap up the event. Once the speaker has given their presentation, there's no need for anyone else to get on stage. Let the speaker handle closing the event by encouraging the audience to visit the sales table.

Also, leave the speaker's microphone on until he tells you to turn it off. Yes, he knows that it's still on. He knows that he's talking to members of the audience while walking to the back of the room and everyone can still hear what he's saying. If he's a good speaker and salesperson, he's using this time, even at the back of the room when his presentation appears to be over, to close more sales.

The only exception to this rule of leaving the mic on is if the event is completely over for the evening (or you've gone on break for lunch during a Saturday workshop), and the speaker leaves his mic on while going to the bathroom. No one wants to hear that over the speakers. (If this last paragraph was a text message, this is where I would write "LOL"!)

By the way, that whole "going to the bathroom with the mic on" thing actually happens. You can laugh all you want, but many of best speakers out there have done it—once. They learn quickly!

Be Prepared

One of the most important things to do is make sure your sales staff is prepared. They need to be ready for the onslaught of customers as soon as the presentation is over. Many speakers are contagiously enthusiastic and are able to send the entire audience to the back of the room. We have both personally had event leaders come up to us and say they've never experienced anything like the sales rush we delivered.

We recently did an event where the only thing we were allowed to sell was a low-priced, low-ticket item, so we ended up selling one of our Lifeonaire books for $20 each. I was speaking to a room of only 100 people and somehow managed to sell 120 books. The staff had no idea that we would sell this many, even though we warned them over and over again that there was going to be a mad rush at the end of the night.

There were so many people crowding around the products they needed to push the tables back to accommodate everyone. The last thing you want is for people to have to wait around to give you their money. The longer they have to wait, the more they have second thoughts about whether they should part with their money and follow through with the purchase. Remember, the confused mind says "no." So does the mind that's forced to wait. Your job is to get them while they're hot. They're ready to give you their money; you should be ready and able to take it.

I was at an event once with about 300 people in the room. I did my close and had them follow me to the back of the room, and I stood on a chair behind the sales table and finished closing. Almost 100 people followed me back and the credit cards were flying. The staff couldn't believe it. After the crowd died down and most of the sales were over, there was a husband and wife that came up to me, and they each had a course in their hands. They said, "Larry, we have a problem." I said, "What's the problem?" They told me they needed a refund. I said, "Already? You haven't owned it five minutes." They proceeded to tell me that when I told people to follow me to the back table, there was such a rush that they got separated and ended up on each end of the sales table, and they both bought my course so they needed to get a refund on one of them. Now that's a good problem to have, right? We sold 76 courses that day.

If your group has yet to bring in a good-selling national REIA speaker, your sales staff may be unprepared for this sort of reaction. Some speakers will sell better than others, but I've seen hundreds of thousands of dollars' worth of product sold in less than an hour. A good selling speaker will generate demand, and your sales staff needs to be prepared to fill it.

Have a System

The best way to be prepared for anything is to plan for it. You need to develop a reliable system that your sales staff can use to effectively process all of the purchases. Consider all that needs to be put in place, which includes how customer's questions will be handled, processing payments, and restocking merchandise.

The following is an example of a great sales system:

As soon as the speaker is done, the sales staff is ready to go. There are enough people at the table to handle everything. One or two people will be designated to handle customer concerns, answer questions, and suggest products. It goes without saying that the staff members with the best communication skills should be the ones interacting with the customers.

The payment processing system is key to getting people in and out quickly. As people choose their products and line up to pay, the cashier can become overwhelmed quickly. You need to avoid any sort of problems at this point in the sale, so I always recommend a specific process for this step.

I'll have customers line up when they're ready to pay. A staff member will take their stack of products and keep them together with the customer's credit card. Another person will then process the payments, print receipts, and call out names. The customers can then come back to pick everything up. This keeps the sales running smoothly and helps your sales staff keep track of what they're doing. The key is to get their order form quickly along with their credit card or other form of payment. Do not make your eager buyers wait to give you their money. They're ready to give it to you; you should be ready to process it!

I'm going to encourage you to do something that goes against the grain of what most people will tell you. If at any point in the process you're having a hard time running payments because of a problem with your merchant account processing or even a lack of staff, I would rather see you get the product into the hands of the customer and send them on their way without processing their payment (you can always process payments later) than see them frustrated that the process is taking too long and have them change their mind. When I tell some REIA owners this, many of them freak out, saying, "Yeah, but what if I give them their product and their credit card doesn't go through?" First of all, it happens, but it doesn't happen very often. When it does happen, you do what needs to be done and keep moving forward.

Let's assume you did as I'm recommending. You've given the customer their product, you run their payment later, and the payment doesn't go through because their card is declined. If the customer has already left and gone home, you can always call them up later and get a good form of payment. If they don't have another form of payment and no other way to make good on their purchase, you simply ask them to return the course. Most of them will give you another form of payment and your problem is solved. If they don't ever answer the phone again or choose not to return the course, they're not allowed back to any REIA meeting again. That alone is deterrent for most people and will get them to return the course. For the most part, 99% of the payments are going to go through. There is that other 1% of payments that aren't going to go through, of which 99% of that 1% of people will make good on their payment and give you another way to process. For the remaining 1% of 1% leftover, yes, someone may get the better of your REIA and end up with a free course. This by far will cost you less over time than the sales you'll lose out on if you make people wait in line for half an hour, waiting for their credit cards to be processed because you either don't have a system in place or are having issues processing payments.

Developing an effective system for the sales table is vitally important. People will be rushing over there, eager to purchase products. If your staff doesn't know exactly what they're doing it can be disastrous. Think of it like any retail situation. People will leave a store if the line is too long. They will be reluctant to purchase something if the store is a mess. Problems with one customer's payments will drive other customers away—it's like cancer spreading throughout the line of people. That will cost you big time. Anything you can do to speed up the process and make it easy for your customers is going to pay huge rewards.

When To End The Event

One of the questions I often get asked is about when to end the event. If you're renting a location then you'll likely be under some sort of time constraint. Even if you aren't worried about getting the room cleaned out, you should know when to end an event. This can be just as important as when to start it.

• After The Speaker

The most obvious answer is to end the event when the keynote speaker is finished. This will be followed by the processing sales and getting the product into the hands of the purchasers. After that, the event is finished and people will go home. The speaker should always be last. I can't stress this enough. They are the purpose of the event and the reason people are sitting in the audience. Anything said after the speaker's presentation will have very little positive impact on the evening. Negative impact, possibly, but not positive impact at all.

• Time

Time is another important consideration. A lot of REIA groups will hold their events after 5 pm because many of their members will be at work during the day. This may not be true for weekend events, but time is still a consideration. What I've found to be consistent all over the country is that no event should go on past 9 pm as previously mentioned. People have a number of different obligations. They might have babysitters to deal with, spouses to come home to or they might have a long commute. Those that have full time jobs are just going to be tired at the end of the day. Some are going to be eager to head over to the local bar or restaurant with their real estate investor buddies to hang out and have some fun. In my experience, 9 pm is when people begin to leave whether the event is over or not. All the more reason to make sure the speaker is able to get started at the appropriate start time, so he can also end on time.

• When Sales Are Finished

If your event was really successful, it's likely that you're going to have people hanging around afterward. There's nothing wrong with this, since REIA members love to network, but at some point you're going to need to get people out of the room. Equipment needs to be broken down, sales need to be tallied, and the room will have to be put back the way it was. Try to give people a reason to head out of the room once they're done buying products. Let them know the event is finished. You may even encourage them by mentioning where a lot of members hang out afterwards. "We usually go to the restaurant down the street after meetings if you'd like to come hang out with us!" If they'd like to network or speak with the group leaders, give them information about your regular meetings.

Your speaker is likely going to be bombarded with questions from the audience at this point in the evening as well. It's important for someone at the REIA to act as somewhat of a gatekeeper during this time, to make sure that any questions taking place immediately after the speaker gets off stage are relevant to purchasing the course or product first. After these people are handled (so they can purchase product), then answering other random questions can be addressed. If this sounds harsh, it's not meant to be that way, but every REIA has that one guy that wants to pick the speakers brain for an hour after the event, and pays no attention to the other people that have questions that will determine their buying decision. It's important, if at all possible, to have someone around that can help the speaker deflect some of these more general questions until other people that need something simple answered so they can make a buying decision can be taken care of.

I can count on it like clockwork; every time I speak, as soon as I get off stage there are people waiting with questions. Sure enough, one guy has a whole list of questions about how to run his real estate business (which I'm happy to help with, but now is not the time), and there is another handful of people around that want to buy the product but have questions like, "Can I bring my spouse to the event?" or "You said you have a money back guarantee, right? Does that timeframe start today?" or "Can I break my payments up into two payments?" These types of questions are coming from people that want to buy the product. They're ready to go for the most part, but may have one small questions or objection to overcome before making their final decision. If I'm off spending an hour with the guy who has questions about how to run his real estate business and these prospective buyers have to wait until I'm finished doing a free coaching session, there's a pretty good chance I'm going to lose those sales.

Listen, I don't mean this wrong. Please don't take these last few paragraphs as a lack of caring for others' needs. My heart wants to help everyone in that room, and truthfully, I'll stay as late as I need to stay to help every single person in that room however I can possibly help them. I've been known to stay answering questions until 2 and 3 o'clock in the morning out of my desire to help. But I must get the sales taken care of first. That's why I was invited to speak. That is one of the keys to the purpose of my presentation, to help provide income to the REIA. I'll help everyone else, but let's get business taken care of real quick first. Anyone that you can put in place to help facilitate this process with the speaker is going to help increase your sales. Trust me; there is always at least one person that has absolutely no sense of sensory acuity to others in the room. This person often forces his way to the speaker and dominates the speaker's time for his own agenda, not realizing that the speaker has an agenda that must be met first.

At this point your event is over, and if you've followed the suggestions in this book, it was a big success. This is no easy feat. You should take the time to be proud of your accomplishments after every event. Now that the audience has gone home, however, you still have a bit of work to do. The next chapter will cover everything you'll need to do after the event. This is just as important as anything we've already discussed, since there are many things that can have both positive and negative effects on your REIA, even after the fact.

Review Questions For Chapter 5

Before the Speaker's Session:

☐ Have you introduced the group and the topic of the event?

☐ Is the audience familiar with everyone who will be on stage?

☐ Have you made sure to get everything out of the way before the speaker comes on?

☐ Did you leave at least 90 minutes for the speaker's presentation?

Introducing the Speaker:

☐ Have you selected who will introduce the speaker?

   Are they:

☐ Familiar to the group?

☐ Respected by the group?

☐ Enthusiastic on stage?

☐ Have they memorized the bio/intro?

☐ Have they practiced the introduction?

Sales:

☐ Is your sales staff ready to go as soon as the speaker is finished?

☐ Have you developed a system to keep things moving smoothly?

☐ Does every member of the sales staff understand their job?

Chapter 6:

After The Event—Make Sure The Audience Never Forgets And Tells Everyone!

The event was a huge success! The room was packed, everyone loved the speaker, and you sold a lot of products. At this point, many would think their work is done. Stopping now is one of the most common mistakes I see REIA groups make. Most REIA owners fail to promote anything that took place at the meeting, leaving money on the table by neglecting continued sales. In this chapter, I will explain exactly what to do after the event to maximize the value of your speaker.

Updating The Website

Remember, your REIA group's website is the most powerful promotional tool you have. All of your other promotional efforts will link back to this site. You should think of it as a value-increasing asset. Every time your group does something, you should mention it on the website. This creates an impression of the group as an active, exciting collection of like-minded people. Remember, no one wants to come back and visit your site if it hasn't been updated in three months.

One of the best things you can do is include plenty of information about recent events. Whenever you hold an event of any kind, you should have at least one person taking professional quality photos. It doesn't have to be a pro photographer. Obviously, the better the pictures look, the more professional your group will look, but any pictures look better than no pictures. They paint a great picture to show the rest of the world how active your group is and how much fun the events can be.

The photos should focus not only on the speaker but on the audience as well. The goal is to help people imagine themselves at the event. A good picture can say more than pages and pages of written text. If you're neglecting to take pictures at your events, you're basically ignoring one of the most effective forms of communication available to you.

Videos are even more effective than photos. While you may not want to post a video of the entire presentation, a montage of short clips can be a great way to build interest in your group. These videos are wonderful promotional tools and can be created with very little effort. A short video clip can be viewed quickly and will deliver a significant amount of information regarding your group. Think of this video as a commercial. It's designed to show how great your events are in only a few seconds.

Speaking of commercials, video testimonials of the event are worth their weight in gold and are about the best commercials you could ever ask for! Having a videographer walk around after an event with a camera works well. It doesn't have to be professional. You don't have to solicit testimonials, nor do you have to have special lighting, a camera crew, special microphones, etc. All those things are great, but just keep it simple. Just have a guy with the camera walk right up to people that attended the meeting and ask questions. Here are a few questions he may ask:

–"What was your favorite part about tonight?"

–"What's one thing you learned tonight that you think will make a difference in your business this year?"

–"What did you like most about the featured speaker tonight?"

–"What kind of person could have benefitted from being here tonight?"

–"Who would you recommend attend one our REIA meetings?"

–"What are some of the greatest attributes of the people at our local REIA?"

Posting videos like this to your site will create a buzz that you simply can't create on your own. It's always better for someone else to tell people how great you are, than for you to tell them.

Featured Article

The first thing you should do, after the event, is update your REIA group's website with these photos and videos. Make sure they are prominently displayed. Some groups have made the mistake of burying this material on some rarely visited page where it's displayed with little to no information. The photos and videos should be one of the first things visitors see when they arrive on the site, and the main page of your site should be updated constantly!

Think about it, why do people come back to a website like Facebook so often? It's because the home page looks different and new every single time you log in. There's always new stuff; it's always exciting to see something new. Your website should be the same.

Consider writing a short article about the event. You can mention things such as the topic of the event or the number of attendees, who benefitted, and how they benefitted from the information shared. Include the photos and videos in this article and make sure to give them some context. If there is a photo of people doing a group activity, for example, mention what they're doing and what the benefits were of the activity. People love this stuff!

You can even make the article a featured article which is displayed on the front page of your group's site. Many modern websites have a slide show which cycles through featured content. This is a great way to give prominence to this material and ensure that visitors have no problem finding it. It's perfectly acceptable to be a little congratulatory in the article. You have, after all, put in a lot of work to make this a successful event.

If you need a little help with this, ask the speaker to help you. He may already have an "After the Event" article he can share, leaving much less work for you to do on your own.

Link To It

In a previous chapter, I mentioned how important it is to utilize social media to help promote your group. One of the reasons an article about the event is so useful is that you can link to it on all your social media accounts. Sites like Facebook will let you link to a specific article and will even include a small blurb when you do. This is a great way to stay in contact with thousands of different users, and get the word out with just a few clicks.

In addition to this, the people who attended the event can also share the link. If you're putting pictures in your Facebook posts, you can tag the people in the pictures from your REIA meeting. This is another great way to spread the word. People love pictures, and sharing them is a non-abrasive form of free advertising. Many of them will be excited to talk about the event they just attended. By posting to Facebook and other social media sites, linking to the article, photos, and videos, you're giving them the ability to share this with all of their contacts. A personal endorsement by a trusted individual is one of the best things you can hope for, making this is a great way to leverage your attendees to help build interest among their family and friends. By the way, every time someone posts an awesome message or testimonial on Facebook, you should copy that right over to your website as well. You'll be surprised how fast word gets out when you let others be a part of sharing the message!

Building The Future

There is a very simple reason why your group should get in the habit of posting photos and videos of past events. Prior success breeds future success. One of the biggest problems facing a brand new business is the lack of prior success. People will always be skeptical of anything new; they want to know they're making a wise decision. The decision to give a business their hard-earned money will often come down to proof of prior success.

The exact same thing is true for REIA groups. People may be interested in your group or the events you hold, but they will be skeptical if they have to go in blind. Anyone who is thinking of attending one of your events will want to know how the past events turned out. They want to make sure they're spending their time and money on a legitimate, valuable option.

As your group continues to hold events and you continue updating your website regularly, it won't take long before you have a mountain of proof showing that people love attending your events. When someone unfamiliar with your group finds the website they will quickly be convinced to attend a meeting or event, not because you said it was so good, but because so many other people said it was so good. This marketing concept has been used by advertisers for decades.

Following Up

Throughout this book I've made the suggestion to collect contact information from the people attending your events. Hopefully, by now it's obvious that the main reason for this is so you can create a relationship with your audience by continuing to follow up even after the event. Getting feedback from the audience is a great way to discover areas of improvement that are needed. If you aren't collecting this contact information and following up, you will simply be assuming things went well. You'll never know for sure.

One of the best things to do after an event is call the attendance list. This will give you the opportunity to speak directly with members of the audience in an environment where they feel comfortable being honest. People in general have a tendency to seek approval. If you ask them about the event in person, while they're surrounded by other people, they may not give an honest answer.

If calling up everyone that attended just seems like an overwhelming and time-consuming task, consider the next best thing. Email them a survey asking for their feedback and suggestions. People love being a part of something. They love being asked their opinion, and they love being the one who came up with the idea that was implemented at the next meeting. It gives them a sense of significance and contribution to the group. Plus, a lot of times they have really great ideas!

The one thing to keep in mind if you're going to survey your audience is to take some of the feedback with a grain of salt. It's easy to hear one complaint out of 200 people and instantly think you need to change everything you're doing to make that one person happy. If you're anything like me, sometimes it's easy to forget about the 199 other people that had great things to say about what you've put together and only focus on the one negative person (who usually complains about everything anyway). Don't let this happen! Just because one person has something to say doesn't make it ironclad, nor should you make immediate drastic changes to your REIA overnight because of this one person making one comment. If you hear a complaint from 50 people out of 100, chances are you've got a legitimate problem. Hearing about a problem from one person out of 100 probably means it's not that big of an issue. Don't make a mountain out of a molehill.

REIA must provide the speaker with a list of all customers that purchased right away. Important!

Don't forget to make sure the speaker got a list of anyone that purchased the course the day or evening of the event. If you've done what we've instructed you to do in this book, you've already given the speaker one of the triplicate order forms from each order immediately after the event ended. If you have a different system in place, do not forget this step. There are some REIAs that are converting to digital ordering systems where each member of the REIA gets a little keychain card with their member information built into it. In these case, members that purchase products at the end of a presentation simply walk up to the back table, hold their REIA card up to a scanner, and the system automatically charges the card on their file for the amount of the sale. We'll likely start seeing more and more of these in the future. In this case, there is no three-part order form; everything was done electronically. This makes it imperative that the selling speaker gets copies of the customer information. Remember, if a speaker has promised to deliver any part of his offer at a later date and people don't get updated with this information right away, you're going to start seeing product returns.

I spoke at an event once a couple of years ago and sold approximately 30 home study course/bootcamp packages at $1997 each, totaling close to $60,000 in sales in a ninety-minute presentation. The promoter in this case failed to get me a list of the customers and sent the customer list in a printout with my check from the sales instead—more than thirty days after the event. I sent numerous emails requesting this information and even had this as a requirement in the contract we agreed to before the event. The final report showed only about $40,000 in sales instead of the $60,000 in sales we really did that night. The reason for this is that ten people requested returns when they didn't hear from anyone within ten days or so after the event. That is not what I promised from the front of the room. I promised people would get an email from me within a few days explaining how to get access to me personally, access to my coaching calls, access to additional online training, a user name and password, etc. When they didn't get this as promised, the purchasers got scared and asked for a refund. Not only did this one foolish failure to follow through cost more than $20,000 in revenue, it also made me and the REIA look bad. Needless to say, I was not a happy camper, and I will not speak for that particular organization again.

Get That Extra Sale!

Following up can be a great way to get honest feedback, but it is also another sales opportunity. When you're speaking with someone who really enjoyed the event, they will naturally get back into the emotional state they were in during that event. They might start telling you how much they enjoyed the speaker or how great the products are. This is a wonderful time to suggest other, possibly related, products they might be interested in.

Let's say you offer a three-book course on investing in real estate. The person you're speaking with may have purchased the first book, simply to see how good the course is. If they've read it and enjoyed it, you have the perfect opportunity to suggest the next two books. While an event can often be loud and chaotic, a one-on-one phone call gives you the chance to really promote this course in detail. This approach is obviously far more effective than simply sending out an email.

This is very different from cold calling. You already know the person was interested because they attended the event. If they've purchased a few products, you know they are willing to spend money on their continuing education. If they enjoyed the products they purchased, you can be sure they're interested in related products. A follow-up phone call is simply a wonderful opportunity to increase sales related to the event. Yes, it takes time to make these calls, but the additional revenue these calls will generate will be more than worth the effort. Plus, I can almost guarantee that none of the other REIAs in your area are doing this. It's just one more thing that sets you apart from other REIAs in your area.

Who Should Follow Up?

There are a couple of options when it comes to follow-up calls. If time is your biggest enemy, you don't always need to do the calling yourself. Many groups will choose to do it themselves, and if you're going to go this route, I would suggest having prominent members of the group do it. If the person making the calls was also one of the people on stage during the event, they will have a much easier time pulling in additional sales. The person they call will be impressed that someone who was on stage took the time to personally call them.

This is a special, personal touch that people will not usually expect. Most people are used to dealing with faceless corporations who utilize call centers staffed with people who could care less. When they receive a phone call from one of the biggest members of your group, however, they can't help but take notice. They aren't used to this level of personal interaction and it will really stick with them.

The problem some groups face is their events are just too darned big to give that personal attention. What a problem to have, right? The attendance list may include hundreds of people and the group leaders simply don't have the time to personally call each person. Fortunately, some speakers will offer to handle the follow up for you.

I actually have a dedicated team of people in my office in Lake Wylie, SC who handle this process. There have been plenty of cases where the REIA group leaders asked for my help to take care of following up with the attendees. In this case, I'll utilize my trained staff whose job it is to call up each and every person, talk to them about the event, then help them get started with the product they purchased and to close sales to the ones that didn't purchase at the event (as long as I have the attendee list). Naturally, I would never charge for this service because it's an opportunity for both me and the REIA to increase sales and make even more money together. And we still split the proceeds just like at the live event.

Don't be afraid to talk with your speaker and ask if they can help follow up with people who attended the event. Not every speaker will have a team of people who can handle it. Speakers like us have made speaking at REIA events a significant portion of our business, but some speakers will simply be too busy. Either way, make sure you're absolutely clear on who will handle this process. It doesn't set a very professional atmosphere when one REIA member gets a call from three different people in your organization asking the exact same follow up questions.

Contacting Your Opt-In List

As we discussed in chapter two, your group's website should be helping you build an extensive list of email addresses. These will be people who are interested in your group and the information you present. It doesn't matter where they live. Most will be close to where your group meets, while others will simply be interested in any online information.

After the event, don't be afraid to send out another email to your list letting them know how awesome the event was. This will serve two purposes. First, it will keep the event fresh in the minds of those who attended it, encouraging them to stay in contact and attend the next event. Secondly, it will give those who missed the event a chance to keep up and see what they missed out on.

When you contact your list after the event make sure to promote the speaker. Even though the event is over, you can still leverage the speaker to help promote your group while potentially increasing sales at the same. Rather than simply mentioning the speaker, you should include an affiliate link (supplied by the speaker).

Often, I'll even create a custom video after I've spoken at an event for the REIA to send out to their list. The video will remind them of what they learned, remind them to take action on a few of the things we've talked about, and even mention that there are two courses left and we'd rather not ship them back. I might even give them a deadline in the video, suggesting that they can only get the deal offered if they take advantage of it in the next 48 hours; otherwise, we're sending the last two courses back. This alone will often get a few people to step up and place an order.

The Affiliate Link

An affiliate link is a sales tool. If you have a website about bicycles, for example, you can post affiliate links to companies that sell bicycle parts. Since these are relevant products, your visitors are likely to click on the link. When they do, they may purchase something, and you will receive a commission on that sale. All of this is handled by special coding so you don't need to do anything more than post the link.

An opt-in list is a wonderful place to use affiliate links. Because everyone on the list is interested in the same subject, you can be sure the products are relevant. People will often open emails right away so it can also be a great way to make some sales quickly. Most speakers will have an affiliate program set up, so you should make use of it whenever you can.

When you contact your mailing list about the event, be sure to include a link to your speaker's websites or products. If your list is large enough, it's a safe bet that a lot of them didn't attend the event. Including this link in the email gives them the chance to check out the speaker and possibly purchase the same products that were available at the sales table. When they do, you'll make a commission from the sales whether they order today or many months from now. You might as well get paid on these additional sales!

The Evergreen Webinar

Another highly under-utilized yet incredibly valuable tool you should be implementing is what's known as "The Evergreen Webinar." This is essentially a pre-recorded version of the same presentation the speaker gave at your event. It will not, of course, be exactly the same, but it will cover the same topics as well as some of the same information. We call it "Evergreen" because it is always useful, no matter when someone may hear or see it, and you can use it year round.

This webinar is a wonderful resource and many speakers will have one. In most cases, access to the webinar is restricted. Visitors will either need to purchase access or submit their email address in order to register see it. Since you're working directly with the speaker, you can offer unrestricted access to everyone on your email list. If you mention that access to this webinar is exclusive to your subscribers, it will be even more enticing.

No matter how well you promote an event, some people simply will not be able to attend. This doesn't mean they're not interested in attending, it just means they couldn't be there for one reason or another. Linking to this webinar is a great way to let those people see and hear the information presented at the event. More importantly, it's also a great way to get sales from someone who was unable to attend in person.

One of the things I have noticed, especially when it comes to having the REIA group host webinars, is that usually a non-profit group has to get "board approval" before hosting a webinar—especially if the webinar is not done right after the live event. The problem with this is that when the Program/Education Director goes to the board meeting and presents the idea of hosting a webinar, that's when things fall apart and the "board" can never make a decision. I would suggest for non-profits to give their Program/Education Director the authority to make those decisions so it doesn't slow down the process or kill the idea up front. You have put someone in that position that you trust to make good decisions, so let them run with it. Now back to the webinar process.

How it Works

You send out several emails inviting your opt-in list to attend a free follow-up webinar put on by the speaker. The speaker will have the email copy already written for you. The link you use to send subscribers to the webinar will be an affiliate link so the speaker can track the people you've referred to their site. It follows the same basic structure of their real world presentation in that it ends with a product offering and sales pitch.

These webinars are created in such a way as to give the feeling of a live event. They may only be accessible at certain times. During these times there might be people available to answer questions or even interact with the attendees. The webinar will make use of pictures, video, and audio to deliver its information. It is essentially as close to being at the event as someone can get from the comfort of their own home.

At the end of the webinar the speaker will then promote their products. They will likely use a free promotional item just as they would at the live event. When the audience purchases one of their products, the affiliate link will ensure you make a commission. This means it's a wonderful way to potentially make some extra money from people who didn't even attend the event.

The best part about this webinar is you hardly have to do anything to make use of it. All you need to do is send out the emails, include the link and send it off to your opt-in list. This is such a simple process there really is no reason to neglect it. The sales made through the webinar can actually be a significant portion of the profits made from an event.

We do this many times as a follow up after I speak at a group. In fact, we can take it one step further. Remember my team in my office in Lake Wylie that follows up with the attendees? Well, I have them call every webinar attendee as well to follow up and make even more sales for the REIA group and me. Is this great or what?

Paying The Speaker

Different speakers will have different payment expectations. It's important to clearly understand what these expectations are before booking them. Even though all speakers will need to be paid at some point, most are willing to wait, and the truth is, they should wait. A speaker that demands to leave the event with a check in their hand is probably not the right speaker for you. That is, unless the speaker is only being paid a flat fee to speak and had no product to sell. In most cases, professional REIA speakers will wait at least thirty days before they expect payment.

The reason for this is actually quite simple. Sales made at the event only account for a portion of the overall sales related to your group's interaction with the speaker. If you've followed the suggestions detailed in this chapter, your group has probably managed to add a few more sales to the books. Some groups may have done a significant amount of digital marketing and will be able to pull in an impressive number of post-event sales.

A good speaker will also create an intense sales period at the actual event itself. Many people will become caught up in the moment. They're still excited from the speaker and will be strongly motivated to put some of the information to use. These people will often purchase quite a few products from the sales table. It's important to remember, however, that many of these products can be quite expensive.

While a book may only have a small price tag, some of the bigger items (such as courses) can represent a significant investment. The customer will, of course, be getting a valuable return when they purchase these items, but they also may have been somewhat impulsive when they purchased it. It isn't uncommon that someone gets home and realizes they bit off more than they can chew. Perhaps their spouse wasn't happy with the purchase, or the customer simply realized they don't have the time to follow through with the implementation of the course as originally intended.

Every good product should have a return policy. This helps to instill trust in the customers and proves the product is legitimate. Some people will offer a full refund with no limitations at all. Others may place a restriction of time or use on it. No matter what the specifics may be or how good the product and speaker is, don't be surprised to see a few returns. When these returns are for big-ticket items, often costing $1,000 or more, it can noticeably affect your overall profits.

This is why it's important to wait a few weeks before paying the speaker. If they have good post-event resources for you to make use of, they will likely be expecting at least a few additional sales. They should also understand the inevitability of returns. If you pay your speaker too early, you run the risk of either paying them too much or too little. You'll then have to spend additional time going back and forth, tallying up the new numbers. It's usually best to just do the final payout after the refund period has expired and all sales have been accounted for.

Let's say, for example, you pay the speaker a week after the event. Two weeks after the event, you see two returns for products costing $1,000. Since you've already paid the speaker based on the pre-return sales figures, you will be paying these refunds out of pocket. Always make sure you have an accurate view of the sales before writing your speaker a check.

One of the things we do, and we actually have it in our contract, is that I want to personally contact everyone who requests a refund. So if the REIA group gets a refund request, they contact my office and I personally call the student. I start out by saying something like this: "Hi. This is Larry Goins and I wanted to personally give you a call to see if there is anything I can do to help you get started." At some point they will tell me they want a refund. Then I go to work trying to save the sale. If I cannot save it I will then find out what they want to do in real estate. I usually end up saying that I have a different program that I think will fit their needs better and I would like to offer it to them for free just to keep the original program. I do this to show them that I am serious about helping them and earning their business. I will usually give them a webinar link to view the presentation for the new product and tell them to call or email me after they watch it and let me know if they want that program. I also never charge the REIA group for the cost of the additional course or shipping or anything. I consider it a cost of doing business, and I have just saved a sale for both the REIA group and myself. It works most of the time.

Pay On Time

This waiting period does, however, need to be agreed upon before the event takes place. It is vitally important that your speaker understands why they need to wait, as well as how long they will be waiting. Try to come up with a set amount of time. Thirty days is a good standard to go by. After this period of time has passed, not only is it unlikely that you will see any additional sales or returns, most REIAs and speakers alike don't offer more than a thirty-day return policy anyway.

Remember, just like REIA owners get together and talk, so do speakers. When speakers get together and talk, they are going to ask their peers for their unfiltered opinion on the groups they've spoken for. If payment was late or sales were handled poorly, this information speaks loudly and travels quickly.

A well-run REIA group's reputation will become well known among speakers. A poorly run REIA group's reputation will also become well known among speakers. Whether your reputation is known as good or bad is entirely up to you. If everything was handled poorly, your group will have a very hard time pulling in high quality speakers in the future. Paying on time and organizing everything in a professional manner, on the other hand, will actually make it incredibly easy to book even the most popular speakers. As a matter of fact, you may even find them calling you!

Do You Have What It Takes?

By now, it's our hope that this book has given you more than just a few suggestions on how to run a highly profitable, highly successful and well-respected organization. All of the suggestions provided work, and all of them have been compiled entirely based on real world experience. That being said, it's easy to sit in your La-Z-Boy recliner and read a book about what to do, it's quite another thing to put these suggestions to work. Out in the real world, there's no way to predict what might go wrong. It can also be just as hard to predict what will be incredibly effective.

Because of this, I want to encourage you to set aside your preconceived beliefs about what you think will or will not work based on what we've covered in this book, and just get out there and have the guts to try it. If you prove us wrong, we'd love to hear about it, but what we've shared with you is time-tested and has been proven to work at many of the largest associations across the country. The bottom line is, it all works. But the truth is, it's unlikely that you're going to implement all of it overnight. Pick one thing at a time. Don't allow yourself to get overwhelmed. And when you check each new thing off your list, be sure have the next thing you're planning on implementing on the radar and goal list. One of the biggest keys to running a successful organization is constant and never-ending improvement. If you welcome this, you'll experience all of the rewards that come with maintaining and growing a REIA.

You'll change the lives of hundreds if not thousands of people. And you'll even earn a pretty darn respectable income in the process!

Review Checklist For Chapter 6

Updating the Website:

☐ Do you have pictures from the event?

☐ Do you have videos from the event?

☐ Have you posted them on your website?

☐ Are they prominently displayed?

☐ Have you created a brief article which talks about the event?

☐ Have you linked to this article from your social media accounts?

Following Up:

☐ Did you collect contact information from the attendees?

☐ Is your group going to handle the follow up calls?

☐ If so, have you decided who will handle it?

☐ Are they prominent members?

☐ Alternatively, are you going to have your speaker handle the follow-up?

☐ Do they have a team of people who can take care of this?

☐ Do you have information on related products?

☐ Is the person making the calls comfortable with sales?

☐ Can people easily order the new products while on the phone?

Opt-In List

☐ Have you prepared a letter for your email list?

☐ Have you included an affiliate link?

☐ Are you adequately promoting the affiliate products?

The Webinar

☐ Does your speaker have an "Evergreen Webinar"?

☐ Can you offer some sort of incentive, such as free admittance, to encourage people to attend the webinar?

☐ Are you using an affiliate link to send people to the webinar?

☐ Are you promoting the webinar on your opt-in list, website, and social media accounts?

Paying the Speaker

☐ Do you have a set date for payment?

☐ Does this date give you enough time to sort out returns and extra sales?

☐ Will you be ready to pay on the agreed-on date?

☐ Do you have reminders set up to make sure you don't miss that date?

In Closing

We hope you have enjoyed this book and it makes you a lot of money and you are able to help a lot of people in your group become successful. We put many months into compiling and creating this book and we thank you for spending the time to read it. It is one thing to purchase educational material because you can always make the money back, but you can never get back the time you have invested in reading this book, so we sincerely appreciate you spending your time reading it.

You will also find several advertisements from different speakers in this book. We hand selected a few speakers that we know, like and trust to be included in this book. Yes, they did pay to be in the book; however, we wanted to make sure that you had some really great speakers to choose from if you were looking for speakers for your group.

Contact The Authors

For more information or to book Shaun McCloskey or Larry Goins to come and speak at your REIA, host a webinar, get free books, CD's, DVDs, affiliate links, run ads in your newsletter, banners on your website, etc., please contact either of them using the information below.

Shaun McCloskey, Lifeonaire Promotions

Topics Covered: Short Sale Real Estate Investing, Debt Free Real Estate Investing, Lifeonaire Living (How to Create a Business that Serves Your Life), How to Become a Top-Selling National Speaker (and Craft a Killer Presentation that SELLS!)

www.lifeonaire.com
135 Triad Center West
O'Fallon, MO 63376
Office: 314-966-0656 ext. 111
Fax: 314-966-5554

For a FREE copy of a book that will change your entire life, please contact Shaun to learn how to implement the Lifeonaire strategies in your own life and business. If you are a REIA owner, president, or board member, Shaun will send you a copy of the new Lifeonaire book at no charge.

Larry Goins, The Goins Group, LLC

Topics Covered: Wholesaling, automation, marketing, software and websites for investors, seller financing, virtual investing, private and hard money and more.

Courses: Ultimate Buying and Selling Machine, Filthy Riches, Bid Blaster, Ultimate Internet Marketing Machine, Branch Acquisition Management, Hard Money Millions.

www.LarryGoins.com
4607 Charlotte Hwy. Suite 1
Lake Wylie, SC 29710
Office: 803-831-0056
Fax: 803-831-0805
Larry@LarryGoins.com
For bookings contact Kandas@LarryGoins.com

193

My name is Shaun McCloskey and I'm an active investor in the St. Louis area. With a special expertise in Pre-foreclosures and Short Sales, as well as a completely life-changing set of strategies called "Lifeonaire," I have something truly unique and special to offer you and your members.

Whether you've heard of me before or not, I want to assure you I'm not like most "gurus" you may have had to deal with. Here are 7 quick reasons why...

1. I'm not a "pretend" expert. Not only am I still running my own highly profitable real estate business in the St. Louis area, I also have a ridiculously high number of successful stories and students who's lives have been totally transformed as a result of what we teach. We also update our course materials every year, that way your members aren't stuck learning about what worked 10 years ago. We teach what works NOW!

2. My touchstone statement is to always "Give First" (and anyone who knows me will testify that I am extremely committed to this.)

3. "Lifeonaire" is the foundation of everything we teach. In case you haven't heard the word "Lifeonaire" yet, think of the word Lifeonaire kind of like a millionaire, only with a LIFE. Most investors today are overworked, stressed out, deep in debt, and the exact opposite of "free." The Lifeonaire principles we teach are not only life changing, they will also completely blow away your audience with a new way of thinking. Check out the reviews on www.amazon.com from our new book, an Amazon "Best Seller" entitled Lifeonaire. It's changing lives BIG TIME! (Email me directly if you'd to request your very own complimentary copy. It will change your life too!)

4. My training is exceptional I honestly don't want to toot my own horn. But I have to be completely honest in sharing that I've seen them all, and I what I have is THE most comprehensive, easy to consume resource on short sales/pre-foreclosure investing around, bar none. You'll agree when you see it.

5. I've trained many of the nations top speakers Many national speakers have paid me tens of thousands of dollars to teach them how to get the results that I get from the front of the room. Many speakers you already know (who speak and sell well, some of which are in this book...) learned how to so this from my events and training.

6. I have a full blown, ready to implement marketing plan to increase attendance and put butts in the seats at your meetings! One of the biggest complaints I hear about speakers is that they do very little to market and increase attendance. Most just want to show up, sell as much as they can, and leave. I'll share with you a full blown done for you marketing plan which can be implemented easily and could potentially DOUBLE your attendance when I come out and speak to your group. I'll also promote your REIA to my own nationwide email list and customer database as well.

7. <u>I have an impeccable, proven track record and reputation.</u> Feel free to ask around, or I can provide you with a huge list of references from other REIA owners/leaders. I've spoken at most of the largest REIA's in the country, (and been invited back multiple times - That's important!) My sales are exceptional. As a matter of fact, I've been the number one highest grossing/selling and most requested featured speaker at the Rich Dad organization for the past three years – and they have a ton of speakers roll through their organization.

"I originally met Shaun about 3 or 4 years ago when I was in St. Louis. He was just getting started as an investor at that time, but he has since blossomed into one of the best short sale experts in the country. I'm very particular about whom I will work with and put my name behind and I couldn't feel better about backing someone. As I read through his course, it's obvious that this guy knows what he is talking about, and he buys into the same philosophy that I do...NO FLUFF! He truly leaves no stone unturned, and he gives you all that you need to know in a step by step plan. Many people claim that. Shaun actually delivers it, which is why we at FlippingHomes.com have decided to back him as a speaker and true educator in this industry. As always, at FlippingHomes.com, we strive to over deliver, and so does Shaun. Anyone who encounters him will feel the same way.
Steve Cook
Founder, FlippingHomes.com

"Not only did our event with Shaun bring in somewhere north of $80,000 in profits, which was incredible, but our members came away feeling like they had just personally experienced the bar being raised substantially in terms of value and effectiveness in real estate investing education.
If you're looking for someone to speak at your group who will not only sell well, but over-deliver and leave your members writing you thank you notes, then I recommend Shaun highly as one of the top speakers to book this year! I've dealt with a lot of speakers over the years, and Shaun is among the best of the best."
Johnpaul Moses
Founder and 6-Year Past President Memphis Investors Group

"Shaun is phenomenal. He tells it like it is, gives out great information and gets the audience charged up and excited. He is a very honest and straightforward speaker with a complete program that is worth every penny. Prior to having him as our speaker, I actually attended his Bootcamp and was so impressed that he became one of the top speakers of choice to bring to our STREET REIA group. In addition, he was awesome to work with and really helped our group as a partner to make it a HUGE success. He dug in and showed us how things worked by writing and executing on our marketing for the event. You can tell he does exactly what he teaches. We had a GREAT turn out thanks to his participation with us from start to finish. He will certainly be invited to come back next year since short sales are here to stay."
Gary Tretter
President The STREET REIA

YOU DESERVE BETTER.
(and I really mean that)

www.lifeonaire.com   shaun@lifeonaire.com   314-966-0656 ext 111

Anthony Chara
Main Topic:
Apartments/Multi-Family
(Other commercial properties
including, Mobile Home Parks,
strip malls, office buildings,
storage facilities & hotels.)

Contact Information:
303-745-5525
support@SuccessClasses.com
www.SuccessClasses.com
Success Classes, LLC
6860 S. Yosemite Ct., Ste 2000
Centennial, CO 80112

Why not take the same time, energy and money that you're putting into buying a one unit property and buy a 10 unit property? A 20 unit property? A 50+ unit property? I made the switch from SFH's to Multi-Family in 2004 when I received this same advice from one of my mentors.

Now, with over 1400 apartment units and counting, and a total asset value well in excess of $28MM ranging from 14 units in Oklahoma to 410 units in Indianapolis, I have the experience to teach your club members how to buy both small and large apartment complexes to increase their wealth substantially. My motto, "Why buy 1 when you can buy 10!" Don't get me wrong, I'm not suggesting that investors stop buying SFH's. I just want to provide them with another tool for their toolbox to help fill in some of the valleys that many investors experience in between finding their 'next' SFH investment.

"Incredible value for a very thorough education. I highly recommend this seminar to anyone having any interest in owning an apartment complex." Rick B.–Crystal Bay, NV

I teach a 1-Day Workshop and a 4-Day Boot Camp. Both are packed with lots of high quality content that your members will rave about and allow them to take action immediately. I also offer a Home Study Course with software, forms and videos, and a follow -up coaching program as part of the Boot Camp. I want your members to hit the ground running and put the strategies they will learn into action right away.

"I've attended many boot camps all over the country on RE, wealth building and personal development. This has been the most content-driven course without the fluff I've found! Anthony is a wealth of knowledge, a great presenter and approachable. I highly recommend this course if you're serious about investing in apartments." Cheryl F. – Boulder, CO

You can read and/or watch additional video testimonials from my students about what they learned, how they put the information to use and the complexes they've purchased on my web site at *www.SuccessClasses.com*. As a recommended speaker with National REIA, I can provide additional references upon request. I look forward to working with you and teaching your members all about the lucrative world of Apartment/Multi-Family/Commercial investing!

Lease Options? Subject Tos? Creative Financing?
Where Do I Start?

I Am Here to Help!

Wendy Patton is recognized world-wide as one of the most inspiring speakers and best selling authors on "Little or No Money Down" real estate investing. Her real estate savvy, great depth of experience and viable knowledge has helped her in orchestrating the most complete and easy to follow Lease Option & Subject To programs in the US and UK.

Wendy has been investing in real estate since 1985. She owns a Keller Williams Real Estate Office with over 180 Agents, is a licensed builder in Michigan, and a full time real estate investor. Wendy has extensive experience in lease options, subject to's, land development, property management, rehabs, foreclosures, new construction and pre-construction with lease options being her favorites. Wendy loves to teach others and assist them to achieve the same level of success that she has personally experienced. She teaches a 90 minute, 1 day and a 3 day lease option bootcamp.

Wendy also runs the Michigan Real Estate Investors Association and has spoken to other REIAs around the country since 1996. She is a frequent guest at the country's largest REIAs where she is frequently asked to return because of her glowing reviews.

Contact Wendy Patton Today!

248.394.0767   Wendy@WendyPatton.com

197

C. Erica Gunnison, CPM, ARM, Broker

Certified Property Manager/Accredited Resident Manager

With 20 years of Asset Management experience throughout the U.S. I have developed proven systems that will help take Property Owners and Managers to the next level. Your members can benefit from the <u>golden nuggets</u> it took me years to perfect!

- The Do's and Don'ts of Self Managing
- Stop Leaving "your money" on the Table!
- How to Manage the Manager, Even if it's YOU!
- STOP! Don't Sign That Agreement!
- Revenue and Delinquency Management
- What's a Pass Through and Why Should I Bother?
- What is Fair Housing and Should I Care?
- Do You RUB People When You Can?
- Repositioning Assets
- When to Use OPP? (Operating Policy and Procedures)

Assisted both large and small Property Owners/Managers, Equity Partners, Bank REO's, and Institutional Funds in all areas of Property Management. With proven expertise in Multi and Single-Family, Student, Senior, Active Adult, Military, Conventional and Affordable Housing, Commercial Real Estate and Retail Management my clients and students know, <u>I've got all their bases covered.</u>

Available for Consulting, Coaching, Asset Management, Forensic Auditing, Expert Witness Testimony, Recruiting, Teaching/Training, and Development.

www.EricaGunnison.com   **topportfoliomanager@yahoo.com**

It is the lifeblood of your business. Without it your business will suffocate and die.

MONEY and CREDIT
The ULTIMATE Power Strategy!

Since 1996 I have worked with clients and investors with one simple goal: get money and get deals closed. It hasn't always been this easy... but I've developed systems that I teach and train that do this for you:

Personal Credit Repair

- The power of **personal credit repair** turns unqualified prospects into ready buyers so you can get your profits faster and easier.

I teach the exact methods I use to take credit scores for zero to 801 in just 117 days. I unveil suppressed techniques that force credit bureaus to remove negative items, or face thousands in fines. When your credit score is high, you pay less for money. When your buyers' credit scores are high, they are eager to buy so your profits are bigger and faster.

Building Business Credit

- When you have access to **Business Credit**...no longer will you be locked out, relegated to low end deals because you lack access to lots of cash. Now funding can be readily available.

I teach how to build Business Credit in the business name, avoiding the risk and liability that comes from borrowing in your personal name. There are three simple steps to unlocking business credit. By learning from me and using the power of the Business Credit Finance Suite, you can have access to money to fund your deals without begging to borrow from your friend's IRA or taking grandmas to lunch at Olive Garden.

All the positive thinking in the world is irrelevant unless you have access to one simple thing: MONEY. Whether you use your own , OPM, or Business Lines of Credit, the deal doesn't close without a cash infusion. I Can Give you a Credit IV

Alan Cowgill
Topics: Private Lending, SEC Compliance & Real Estate Management
937-390-0816   mkt@acowgill.com
www.PrivateLendingMadeEasy.com

I'm known all over the nation as the guy who cracked the code on **acquiring private lenders** for both residential and commercial real estate deals. Since 1995, I have done hundreds of real estate transactions.

I love speaking at REIA meetings and have created a powerful program where I speak at your evening meeting and cover my Private Lending Made Easy Basic techniques. I then teach a riveting workshop on Saturday where I do additional private lending training and also cover YOUR STATE'S SEC private lender laws to help keep your members SAFE and in SEC compliance.

You should know that at my own live event, using the exact training in my Basic System alone, my students have raised over **a half a BILLION DOLLARS** in the first 24 hours. This is over the life of my live events.   That is just an indication that my private lending training at your evening meeting is a no-nonsense, yet easy to use system. Folks love it.

While I have created more than 50 different products for real estate investors to use, the two main systems I'm ask to teach at REIA Groups are my Private Lending Made Easy System and Business Management Made Easy program. I do this nationally for dozens of REIAs every year.

When I teach <u>my Basic System strategies</u>, folks learn how to obtain private lender funds from amongst their Family, Friends, & Associates, build their credibility and generate leads.

When I teach <u>my Premium System strategies</u>, folks learn how to obtain private lender funds from strangers. Your members are taught how to manage their private lenders, what documents are required, and how to attract the "pot of GOLD" of private money - IRA money.   But many students believe **the most important thing I teach is SEC Compliance**; both state and federal.

One other system I love to teach is my **Real Estate Management Made Easy System** where I show students how to manage <u>the ugly part</u> of real estate investing...business organization.   It isn't SEXY, so other trainers avoid it.   But ALL INVESTORS need it because it's their Achilles Heel. It's how to remove chaos and inefficiency by automating. Including systems in a real estate investor's business can be a turning point in their success. Businesses can fail without this.

My schedule fills up fast. If you need a speaker who delivers solid training, then call NOW.

"Alan spoke to our REIA in September. He was a delight to work with from the beginning. His presentation at the monthly meeting was very well received. As a matter of fact, Wendy Patton and I told him that Thursday's meeting doesn't sell well and don't be discouraged if very few buy but they do on Saturday during the One Day Workshop. I'm glad to say we got to eat crow on that! Alan is now our top producer on Thursday and I will never utter those words again! His One Day Workshop was also very well presented—the members really enjoyed Alan, his thoroughness and he offers great products."

"After the event, Alan's follow up was perfect and his staff, Donna, has been right on top of the details. Alan has been proactive in getting us promotional materials when needed, was incredibly prepared, well respected by the audience, and he has a great product that even I have used with success! Alan will definitely be on our "Welcome Back" list!"

Beth Slade, Executive Director MREI - Michigan Real Estate Investors

Main Topics Joe Presents On:

1) Wholesaling Lease Options -
The fastest way to make large chunks of cash is to flip "Lease Options" to tenant-buyers. Discover why this creative strategy is one of the easiest businesses to automate and outsource.

2) Marketing and Automation -
Learn the three keys to success:
1) Marketing
2) Automation
3) Delegation
We are not in the real estate business. We are in the <u>Marketing Business</u>. Learn all about creating simple systems to get "Marketing Done For You, In Spite Of You".

Joe McCall
Entrepreneur, Author, Podcaster, and Consultant
(314) 266-1221   joe@joemccall.com

Testimonials:

"Joe has presented at several of my events. The attendees always get great content and rush to the back to invest in his training. I highly recommend him!"

- Larry Goins,
Author and Speaker

"I have known Joe McCall for many years. I have seen him speak several times, and he has been thru my speaker training. I consider him a trusted friend & I highly recommend him!"

- Shaun McCloskey,
Author and Speaker

"Joe McCall is one of the most creative and innovative business people I know. Listening to him teach is filled with nuggets that will make someone a better business person."

- Steve Cook,
Lifeonaire

"Joe McCall has presented at OREIA's National Real Estate Summit in 2 separate years. Our experience with him both times was excellent. He's well received, sells well, has a good product, and provides the support he says he'll provide. I highly recommend him as a speaker."

- Vena Jones Cox, OREIA
Convention Coordinator

"Joe McCall has spoke at our REIA twice in the last 4 years, and both times he left the crowd buzzing with all the information he shares. His product is vast, and is constantly being updated. Not only did his customers learn a ton, they have become sources of tips and techniques for our group. I totally recommend getting Joe for a full day workshop!"

- Eric Lundberg,
Owner Milwaukee REIA

REI BLACKBOOK
THE DEAL MAKER ENGINE

Do more **deals.**
Make more **money.**
Have more **time.**

Simplify Technology
Professionally designed websites and landing pages with follow-up email campaigns are **done for you.**

Get Organized
Keep all contacts, tasks, and deals in one place with our fully integrated CRM so you will **never lose a lead.**

Automate Marketing
Save more time from single property websites, flyers, html ads, and instant publishing to 35 third party sites.

Make More Money
Analyze comparables, deal types, scenarios, financial plans, and exit strategies to **find the right deals.**

Get Referrals
Build relationships, partner with investors, discuss questions, acquire properties, and sell your next deal.

FoR a FREE Demo Account
Visit **REIBlackBook.com/REIA**

ASK ABOUT OUR **WHITE LABEL** OPTIONS

I Can Tell You How Great I Am And Why You Should Have Me Speak, But I Think You Would Rather Hear It From Other REIA Owners!

Wendy Patton, MREI— *"Our members absolutely loved Jason Roberts and his presentation on how short sales can work in today's real estate market. He knows how to convey the subject matter he is an expert in it so the audience can understand it and implement it."*

Kim Tucker, MAREI—"*With Jason Speaking at our larger meeting and sharing his story about where he came from and how he turned his life around through real estate, we were able to set a record attendance at our Saturday Training."*

Steve Love, Prosperity Through Real Estate— *"At the Saturday workshop, with 80 members in attendance, Mr. Roberts sold 20 courses priced at $2000 a piece. With a 25% selling rate and rave reviews from many of our members, its only fair to say that Jason Roberts was a massive hit."*

Eric Lundberg, Milwaukee REIA— *"What an amazing experience! I LOVED it for many reasons—first, his open demeanor and personal story really resonated with my members— new and experienced alike. Two different people— who still had no interest in short sales— came to me after his presentation and told it was the BEST speaker I've had since they joined. Rarely do I hear that about a selling speaker! Second, he talked about Short Sales in a way only a super experienced operator could speak— he was able to share tips, insights, and work—arounds that the active shortsalers liked and wanna-bes actually understood."*

Book Jason To Speak
From Bankruptcy to $3.6 Million In Just One Year

Jason is one of the top speakers in the country on Real Estate Investing. In 2010, Jason lost his home to foreclosure, cars repossessed, and even had to file a personal chapter 7 bankruptcy. Can somebody really invest in real estate in the middle of being completely wiped out? Let me assure you, it can be done. We've all heard the stories from GURUS about how to make money in real estate with no money down, no credit etc. Jason was about to put it to the test. Jason flipped over 100 homes home for just shy of $3.6 million dollars in profit, and hasn't shown any signs of stopping since!! And the best part about it is, he does this in about an hour or two a day and is willing to show you how too! Jason now spends most of his time living out his vision and helping others do the same through personal coaching and business consulting.

www.bookjasonroberts.com

314.369.7645

jason@lifeonaire.com

INVESTORS REHAB

Invite Larry Goins' Buying & Selling Team
To Your Next Group Event!

→ **Team Members Available to Speak at Your Group (Content Only Training)**

- Proprietary techniques used to negotiate & obtain deep discounted properties not available to the public.

- Investing and wholesaling for over 20 years.

- Proven track record quality investment opportunities

→ **Earn $$$ by Offering Wholesale Properties to Your Members** (The group will get **PAID** for houses sold to your members!)

- Property ads in your Newsletters

- Banners on your website for wholesale properties

To Check Availability for Your Next Meeting or Discuss Advertising Opportunities...

Contact: Gaby
Gaby@InvestorsRehab.com
803-701-1006

"Discover How to Master Fear, Doubt & Frustration, Make Better Decisions & Enjoy Consistent High-Quality Results in Your Business & Life"

"Doug's very professional, and super easy to work with. The presentation was excellent and sales were great too! He stayed and gave several hours extra to the buyers of his system, I've never seen anyone do that." ~ *Jack Bosch. Orbit Investments, Phoenix, AZ.*

"Amazing! Our members responded very well. Doug is so professional, you can reach him and he responds to your emails! He showed up on time and stayed late, and gave a lot of extra time to our people and that's why we're getting rave review." ~ *Tom & Carolina Zeeb, Traction REIA*

One of the most important emotions for both our survival, and our potential demise is "**Fear**". Your veteran and newbie investors alike will benefit from Doug's 20 plus years of business and real estate investing experience & helping others master fear in this entertaining presentation where they'll learn:

```
* How to end confusion & create a clear vision for your business & life
* The exact blue print Doug uses to create financial freedom
* How to fast track your way to success
* Learn about the 'hard-coded blueprint' that everyone has and how it holds you back
* How to get unstuck and take action, or move past the plateau to get results
* The top three fears for all real estate investors - based on tons of case studies of
  Doug's Clients and what you can do about these fears once you understand them
* Recognizing when you are slowing down or getting stuck - and what to do about it
* How to tweak your business and your mindset to break through to the next level
```

"Doug's Fun Hypnosis Show sold out our banquet for the first time in 5 years, our attendees were thrilled, oh, and he sold well too. I highly recommend Doug." ~ *Vena Jones Cox, OREIA*

"Doug Ottersberg was so easy to work with, speaker sales were very good and our members loved him!" ~ *Sheila Astley, RICH Club, Houston, TX.*

Since 1994 Doug Ottersberg and his wife Ana have worked side by side raising three children and building their real estate investing business to provide deserving families with quality affordable housing. Their business includes manufactured home communities, single family homes, land, a manufactured home dealership and finance company. Along the way, several failures and an embarrassing moment of truth caused Doug to feel like some unknown force had him in its grip, keeping him from enjoying the successful results he wanted. His journey to help himself launched Doug's mission as a Business and Life Strategist, helping other real estate investors and business owners make better decisions and achieve better results, bridging the gap from frustration to a better quality of life.

"After a few sessions with Doug my income increased $46,000 in one weekend! In addition, I'm now eating healthier, enjoy going to the gym and went from a size 12 to a size 0! What an amazing bonus! Thanks, Doug." ~ *Lindsey J., Temecula, CA*

"Doug not only helped my wife and I get more money coming in the door, he also helped our relationship. I released some old limiting beliefs and watched my sales increase over 400%, and my wife was able to conquer the anxiety that had plagued her for years! She no longer needs medications and hasn't had a panic attack since! " ~ *Edwin K., Las Vegas, NV*

"Years of stress & anxiety were keeping me from closing sales I knew I was capable of. As a result of working with Doug, I can relax and my closing ratio has increased from 5% To 21%!! I was so impressed with my own results I sent my mom to see Doug" ~ *Carolina Z., Washington, D.C.*

Book Doug Today at: 888-321-3684
DougOttersberg.com

SUE NELSON

REONoteProfits@gmail.com - **877-933-0879**
www.REONoteProfits.com

*Sue Nelson
Founder*

Buying From Banks - Commercial Real Estate, REOs, Notes and Super Creative Deal Making!
Regardless of your group member's individual level of expertise Sue Nelson is a perfect choice for your Real Estate based group. She currently has a 100% satisfaction rating among all of the REIA's and investment clubs she has spoken at. Students of every level consistently agree that her presentation is never pitchy but thoughtful, fun and filled with information.

Her course *Buying from Banks – REO's Notes and Super Creative Deal Making* sells at $995 and is simplified but a complete business in a box and something the student can really set out and see monetary success after a short 30 days.

Her sales are very high, on stage as well as on webinars. She is a great educator with great marketing and wonderful follow-up customer service. Everything is done for you and very easy to promote. Sue has spoken Internationally. REIA's from as far as Sydney Australia to the entire United States with REIA's including; Chicago REIA, MIREIA, Prosperity Through Real Estate (LAREIA), CTREIA, NOREIA, MAREIA and many more.

Her personal experience in the business is extraordinary giving her instant credibility and her down to earth nature and passion for the subject is infectious. Sue Nelson and her partners own over 1500 apartment units. She has been called a true transactional engineer as most of these acquisitions have started as note or REO negotiations and everything in between. She was an art teacher for over eight years before her transition to real estate and is now one of the country's leading educators in commercial real estate and note acquisition.

You may be familiar with Sue and her wealth building strategies from her appearances on NBC, ABC, CBS and FOX television. Now she holds nothing back as she brings these closely guarded secrets home to you! Don't miss out on this great opportunity to have one of the best speak on your stage!

Draw Larger Numbers to Your Real Estate Meetings or Conferences!

Jeffrey typically increases attendance at real estate meetings by DOUBLE or TRIPLE the normal numbers.

Jeffrey is America's #1 Landlording Coach. He is available to speak at monthly association meetings, at no charge to the group, or to conduct half day or full day sessions for real estate conferences. He has spoken for hundreds of REIA (Real Estate Investor Associations) landlord, rental owners and apartment associations. In addition he has spoken for NAA, IREM and NARPM local chapters and national conferences.

Founder of MRLANDLORD.COM website, that has over 1,000,000 page views every year, and the most visited Q & A Forum on the Internet by rental property owners where answers and tips are provided by fellow rental owners across North America, professional property managers, CPAs, and real estate attorneys.

Author of bestselling books nationwide on the subject of property management, THE LANDLORD'S KIT and THE LANDLORD'S SURVIVAL GUIDE.

Interviewed on numerous radio talk and TV shows across the country and quoted in hundreds of publications, newspapers and magazines including; CNN, The Wall Street Journal, Smart Money, Personal Finance Magazine, Real Estate Journal, Business Week Magazine, and the New York Times.

Conducted over 1200 seminars and workshops, speaking to more real estate associations nationwide than any other active real estate instructor.

SPEAKING TOPICS INCLUDE:
- Create A Goldmine - How To Create A Huge Monthly Cash Flow With Rental Properties!
- How To Fill Vacancies Within 72 Hours
- How To Keep Residents Longer & Improve Their Performance
- How To Protect Yourself And Your Investments As A Landlord

For sample promotional materials including a video interview, audio clip, fliers, email, press release, etc., go to LandlordingCoach.com. References from association presidents and program coordinators are available upon request.

"Jeffrey Taylor (aka MR. Landlord) has consistently delivered some of the most valuable content on landlording, increasing profits and cash flow. His extensive experience has helped thousands achieve their real estate dreams. His seminars are a unique opportunity... You won't want to miss a minute! He's not only a proven expert that can deliver, he delights his audience with very real and often entertaining anecdotes. After his sessions you (your association members) will be motivated to take on the world of landlording and succeed!"

- RPOA (Rental Property Owners Association)

CONTACT INFO:

P. O. Box 64442
Virginia Beach, VA 23467
Phone: 757-436-2606
Fax: 757-436-2608
editor@mrlandlord.com
www.LandlordingCoach.com

Property Investing Can Be Headache Free!

Tim Grimmett is an active investor and real estate coach specializing in promoting how to safely purchase turn-key properties and rental properties. Tim teaches several different strategies on how to use qualified money from your Roth or Traditional IRA's to fund deals. Tim uses proven systems to encourage debt free investing strategies (loans with a maximum of 7 years) as well as other Lifeonaire Investing Techniques.

Ready to Get Rid of the Pain of Investing?

Contact Tim Today!

Tim Grimmett

Headache Free Properties

314-283-6022

Tim@Hafpinc.com

2166 N. Waterford Drive, St. Louis, MO 63033

213

What Every Real Estate Investor Needs!

Discover Top Investors' #1 Preferred Way to Generate Passive Income Each and Every Month

For real estate investors, rehabbers and busy professionals looking to maximize their return on investments, peer-to-peer lending can be the answer for that new source of income.

MPactWealth's entry level program - The Passive Income Manifesto teaches THE proven formula (used by Bankers) for generating passive income – without being dependent on any single investment asset class or gambling with your own money.

The flagship program - The Bankers Code teaches how generating consistent passive income is easiest to do via private lending using other people's money. This program has set thousands of people on the road to creating wealth and passive income and has been the catalyst to us becoming an Inc. 500 company.

MPactWealth offers powerful free Webinars, video based trainings and downloadable books designed to help individuals grow and thrive financially, building wealth with passive income - we can also present these trainings live at your next event.

We have a generous partner program that is designed to make you money on autopilot.

To learn more about our programs and this lucrative collaboration, call Todd at 925.588.7028 or email Todd@MPactWealth.com.

MPactWealth is the largest network of private lenders in the world. Led by founder George Antone, author of best-selling book, "The Banker's Code," this network works together to provide trusted wealth-building education, implementation training, and a thriving peer-to-peer lending community.

DWAN WITH STEVE FORBES

FOUR-TIME Best-Sellers **Dwan Bent-Twyford**, America's Most Sought After Real Estate Investor™ and **Bill Twyford**, The Real Estate Rock Star™ will rock the house at your next group meeting, keynote speech, webinar or any other event you are planning!

Unlike the run of the mill, cardboard cut-out, suit-and-tie speakers... Bill and Dwan bring down the house with their playful attitudes, their rock-star looks, and 20 plus years of on-the-street real estate investing experience!

They have spoken on stages with Donald Trump, Robert Kiyosaki, Suze Orman, Tony Robbins and many more!

They have been featured on Fox & Friends, MSNBC, Colorado and Company, Naomi Judds morning show, and many more media outlets!

In fact, RealtyTrac® just featured the TOP FIVE real estate investors in the country. Dwan and one of her superstar students, Jim Ferebee, were TWO of the top FIVE!

They cover trending topics such as:

The Real Estate Rock Stars!
www.InvestorsEdgeUniversity.com
303-870-8851
BOOK BILL OR DWAN TODAY!

- ➢ Flipping Foreclosures
- ➢ Short Sales®
- ➢ No Equity Foreclosures
- ➢ Finding Hidden Treasures in Your Own Back Yard
- ➢ Scripts for Homeowners and Banks
- ➢ And much, much more!

You won't find two more entertaining or successful investors for your event!

BILL WITH DAN KENNEDY

Index

Made in the USA
San Bernardino, CA
08 December 2014